MADE IN AMERICA
CHRIS CHELIOS

with KEVIN ALLEN

MADE IN AMERICA
CHRIS CHELIOS

with KEVIN ALLEN

TRIUMPH
BOOKS

This book is available in quantity at special discounts for your group or organization. For further information, contact:

Triumph Books LLC
814 North Franklin Street
Chicago, Illinois 60610
www.triumphbooks.com

Printed in U.S.A.
ISBN: 978-1-60078-987-8
Design by Patricia Frey
Title page photo courtesy of Icon Sportswire
Photos courtesy of Chris Chelios unless otherwise indicated

To the memory of my sister, Gigi.

−C.C.

To Nate Brown, a Detroit Red Wings fan living openly
among Blackhawks fans in Chicago.

−K.A.

Contents

Foreword

The first time I lined up against Chris Chelios in the NHL, I remember thinking that he wasn't very big for a player who was supposed to be a tough defenseman.

By the time I played my second shift against him, I had changed my mind about how big he looked.

Every time I was on the ice against Chris, I knew I was going to be subjected to in-your-face defending. I made it my business to always know where Chris was when I was playing against his team; I wanted to know if he was in the corner, in front of the net, or drinking Gatorade on the bench. He played a hard, edgy game. He was going to do what he needed to do to win. In that regard, he reminds me of my former Edmonton Oilers teammate Kevin Lowe.

Chris was an honest player. He never cheated on his effort and he respected the game. He used to run me all the time, but I knew that he didn't want to hurt me. He just wanted to win. You have to walk a fine line when you play with the edge that Chris did, but against me, he never crossed the line between clean and dirty play.

"I'm right behind you!" he would yell, just before he clobbered me.

He was particularly effective when he played for the Blackhawks in the smallish Chicago Stadium. You never seemed to have much time to make a play in that building, especially when Chris was always all over you making the situation worse.

But whether Chris was playing in Montreal, Chicago, or Detroit, his only objective was to be a champion. He was the ultimate team guy.

Chris has an overflowing passion for the game. He played the same way at age 28 and 38 as he did at 48. He played with the same passion in October as he did in May.

Even though we never played on the same team, we are close friends today. Oddly enough, our friendship began during the Canada Cup. Although I played for Canada and Chris is American, we got to know each other through mutual acquaintances. Later, when I ended up in Los Angeles, I was roommates with Tony Granato, and he and Chris are good friends. It was easy to see why. In addition to being Wisconsin alumni, they both played a pesky style and they both have big hearts. It was clear that Tony had unwavering respect for Chris.

What I like about Chris is his honesty. He tells you what he is thinking. He won't lie to you. You know where you stand with him. He's the kind of friend who would do anything for you. If you need help, he's the first guy you want to call.

After he bought a home in Malibu, California, I saw him even more during the summer. My family, particularly my children, always loved his Stanley Cup parties. Chris would park the Cup on the beach and people were drawn to it like metal to a magnet.

My former teammate Mark Messier once said there wasn't a single thing about the game of hockey that he didn't like. He said he loved the travel, the practice, the competition, the camaraderie, talking to the media, and all of the rest that goes into playing in the NHL. That's the kind of passion that Gordie Howe had.

And that's the kind of passion that Chris Chelios had.

All three of those guys were smart, unselfish, Hall of Fame players who played a quarter of a century in the NHL. You had to take away their skates because they wouldn't give them up. They were from different eras, but they were tied together by their passion and their love of competition. Howe, Messier, and Chelios were cut from a different cloth than other players. I believe their longevity stemmed from their passion.

When retired players get together, they always discuss their fond memories of playing against one another. Unfortunately, Chris and I never faced each other in an NHL playoff series. Even though we don't know for sure how that series would have turned out, I have a pretty good idea: Chris would have been out against me every shift, and he would have had that trademark smirk on his face every time he clobbered me.

—Wayne Gretzky

Prologue

t was a scene in a conference room, not on the ice, that cemented my belief that defenseman Chris Chelios is the greatest American-born player in hockey history.

Top American players were showing up one by one to fill out their paperwork in anticipation of the 2002 Olympic Games. As guys started to arrive, each was greeted by hellos and nods. Brian Leetch received extra handshakes. And there was a small commotion when Mike Modano and Jeremy Roenick entered the room.

But when Chelios stepped through the doorway, it was a different story. Modano and Roenick jumped from their seats and greeted Chelios as if Elvis had just entered the building.

It was probably similar to what occurred when Frank Sinatra entered a nightclub in the 1950s. Twenty seconds after his entrance, Chelios was the center of attention. At least 10 players formed a half-circle around him. Stories were told. Barbs were thrown. Laughter was heard.

Not long after witnessing that scene, I wrote a column ranking the top American players in hockey history. It was as if

I had just unlocked the DNA code of the American herd. It was clear to me that Chelios was the binding agent that tied this talented collection of players together. Based on his impact, and the intangibles that were on display at that gathering in Colorado Springs, Colorado, I ranked Chelios No. 1 for the first time.

Many people around the NHL talked to me about that list, and some disagreed with putting Chelios at the top. But no one has ever said to me that Chelios shouldn't be part of the conversation.

The players who rose up to greet Chelios in Colorado Springs constituted America's greatest hockey generation and he was unequivocally the leader of that group. He was the alpha dog of the American program. That would have been clear to anyone who had seen the interaction between Chelios and the American players.

"He is the godfather of American hockey, and I think many of the guys feel that way about him," said Roenick.

Doug Weight once joked that when Chelios was born he entered the world with "sergeant stripes on his arms." He is a natural leader, someone who organizes the team parties and then is first in line when trouble breaks out on the ice.

"If you were in a pillbox and the enemy was attacking, Chris is who you would want in there with you," said Russell Lowell, his friend of more than 30 years.

Some of Chelios' teammates call him "Captain America."

"He stands up to everyone and backs down from no one," said Dallas Stars general manager Jim Nill.

Chelios' accomplishments speak for themselves: an NCAA championship, three Stanley Cup championships, three Norris Trophies (and two-time runner-up), and induction into the U.S.

and Hockey halls of fame as soon as he was eligible. He played on four U.S. Olympic teams, the last one in 2006 when he was 44 years old.

Some argue that Leetch should be the top-ranked player, or even Modano or Pat LaFontaine. Some even argue for Eveleth, Minnesota, goalie Frank Brimsek, who was a star in the NHL in the 1930s and 1940s when the league was almost exclusively a Canadian club.

Brimsek won the Calder Trophy in 1938–39, two Vezina Trophies as the NHL's top goalie, plus two Stanley Cup championships. Although Brimsek played only 10 NHL seasons, his name often appears on lists of the top 100 NHL players of all time.

Michigan native LaFontaine would have had a stronger case if his career had not been shortened by post-concussion syndrome. He was 33 when he retired, and yet still finished with 1,013 points in 865 games.

Seven times, LaFontaine scored 40 or more goals, and six of those came in succession from 1987–88 until 1992–93. The electrifying center registered 148 points for the Buffalo Sabres in 1992–93.

Modano, another Michigan native, is the top-scoring American-born player in NHL history, a divine skater and a magnificent scorer. He finished his NHL career with 561 goals. Anyone who remembers seeing Modano roaring up the ice with the puck will never forget it.

However, it may be Leetch who provides the greatest competition for Chelios. Some believe Leetch is the greatest New York Ranger of all time. He won two Norris Trophies, a Calder Trophy, and a Conn Smythe Trophy as playoff MVP when his New York

Rangers won the Stanley Cup in 1994. He was arguably more dominant and spectacular than Chelios. He could skate end-to-end like an American Bobby Orr. It's impossible to fault anyone who chooses Leetch over Chelios.

But Chelios gets the nod simply because he is Chris Chelios, and everyone who ever played beside him understands what that means.

IN CANADA, MARK MESSIER was the symbol of that country's willingness to do anything in the name of winning. Messier was a savage competitor. The Americans boasted Chelios, a man who was equally relentless. Chelios was a player who loved the game so much he played 26 NHL seasons. He played his first NHL game on March 8, 1984, for the Montreal Canadiens and his last on April 6, 2010, for the Atlanta Thrashers.

In between those dates, he played every game as if he were re-enacting a scene from the movie *Braveheart*.

"He was always a warrior," Roenick said. "If you tried to hit Chelios, you'd end up chewing on his stick. The closer you got to Chelios, the higher his stick would come up. He was the king of the chop. If you violated his personal space, he would chop you across the ankles."

His desire seemed even more important than his considerable skill level. Chelios once scored 20 goals in a season, and registered 70 or more points three times. At one point during Chelios' career, he was a plus player for 10 consecutive seasons. He retired with a plus-minus of plus-350. He was plus-40 in the season he turned 40 years old.

Chelios was a smart, effective quarterback on the power play, a fearless penalty-killer, and a ferocious hitter.

But it was the other traits that separated Chelios from his peers. He played with overwhelming passion, unwavering support for his teammates, and a volcanic intensity that intimidated his adversaries. He was always a bomb waiting to go off. No American player has ever been harder to play against than Chris Chelios.

"He always played above his ability," said his 1984 U.S. Olympic coach Lou Vairo.

That may be the best description of Chelios. Some players don't take full advantage of their talent, while others make the most of their ability. When you watched Chelios, it always seemed as if he was getting *more* done with *less* physical ability.

Chelios was a skilled player with a venomous bite. He was much more physical on the ice than Leetch. He had roughly five times more penalty minutes than Leetch owned.

Although Leetch was considered a leader, the Chelios leadership aura was far more pronounced. Most of the American players in the Leetch-Chelios era viewed Chelios as the player carrying the flag.

Chelios' list of intangibles also includes a durability and longevity that is almost unmatched in hockey history. Only legendary Gordie Howe was older than Chelios when he played his last NHL game. And not even the incomparable Howe played more playoff games than Chelios (266).

Even when Chelios was in college at Wisconsin, it was clear that his incredible stamina set him apart from his peers.

"He wanted to play the whole game," former Badgers coach Jeff Sauer said. "He would take a shift, get off the ice, take a drink of water, and he would stand up and be ready to go again."

His focus was legendary.

"He's the type of person who concerns himself only with the last five minutes he has played and the next five minutes he will play," Sauer said. "He focuses on the moment."

It shouldn't be surprising that the movie *300* is a Chelios favorite. It's the story of a small army of Spartans holding off an overwhelming force of Persians. Former Red Wings teammate Kris Draper started calling Chelios "Sparta" to acknowledge his competitive spirit.

"He had a will about him," said former Detroit teammate Dan Cleary. "If you pick a fight with Chelios, you had better make sure he's gone, because he wouldn't quit."

It is not a coincidence that Chelios played in the NHL 26 seasons and only missed the playoffs twice.

DURING THE 2014 NHL playoffs, Los Angeles Kings coach Darryl Sutter had the luxury of having Drew Doughty in his lineup. Entering the 2014–15 season, Doughty owns two Stanley Cup rings and two gold medals for helping Canada win the Olympic Games in 2010 and 2014.

Yet Sutter still insisted that Chelios is the best defenseman he ever coached.

Chelios went from playing recreational hockey to the NHL in less than five full years. He went from San Diego beer league hockey to junior hockey in Moose Jaw to college hockey at Wisconsin to the Olympics to the NHL at a time when most hockey experts would have said that was an impossible climb, especially in an era when most observers looked down their noses at players from the United States.

"What made Chris special is that a coach only had to tell him once what he needed to do and he would have it down," said former Moose Jaw Canucks teammate Bobby Parker.

Even injuries couldn't derail Chelios' spirit. When he suffered a major knee injury at age 38, he was on the ice not long after his surgery.

"The team was on the road and the arena was dark," said Nill, who was Detroit's assistant general manager at the time. "I heard something and it was Chelios skating down the ice. It wasn't long after his surgery. He wasn't allowed to turn, so he would lift himself on the boards to turn around…. He was by himself. There was no one around to see it."

But Chelios wouldn't have been able to look at himself in the mirror if he hadn't made a Herculean effort to get back in the lineup as soon as possible. That's just who he is. He has a pride in his work that is second to none.

We should all be thankful that Chris Chelios was made in America.

—Kevin Allen

Introduction

I was always thankful that I never played against Wayne Gretzky in an NHL playoff series—not because I didn't like to play against the best, but because I probably would have had to break his hand.

I would not have wanted to injure Gretzky, mind you. I loved the guy. He was our sport's greatest ambassador. He was and always has been a classy person. How could you not like a guy like Wayne Gretzky? That's why I never touched him on the ice in a regular season game. I made every effort to frustrate him but I never attempted to injure him. I had too much respect for how he played and how he carried himself.

That said, I'm sure he believed I wanted to hurt him because I always tried to leave that impression. That's probably why he got caught by that famous check from Gary Suter in the 1991 Canada Cup. As Gretzky and I chased the puck, he was so worried about me smashing him into the boards that he didn't even consider Suter might hurt him from behind.

But I can say without question I would have tried to hurt him if we had been matched up in the playoffs. In my mind, there were no friends in a playoff series. It was survival of the fittest.

I'm not talking about elbowing someone in the head or going after someone's knees. That can cause long-term injury. I'm talking about a strategic slash. To me, slashing someone's hand or breaking someone's fingers was nothing. It was part of the game.

Broken hands heal. Fingers heal. The pain that comes from losing does not.

It's true that I once came into the Chicago Blackhawks dressing room between periods and asked who was going to step up and "break Brett Hull's arm."

Hullie was a good friend of mine, and yet I would have knocked him out under the right circumstances.

Friendships cease to exist in the NHL postseason. That's the way I played. That's the way Mark Messier played, too. I was glad I never faced him in the playoffs either, because I would have had to go after him and he probably would have cross-checked me in the face.

In the 1980s and 1990s, players used to hate each other more than they do today. Guys tried to hurt me when we played. Today, guys are always switching teams and players seem to all know each other more than we did when I was in the prime of my career.

But I didn't need to hate people to hurt them. Hull and I were good friends, but he understood that about me. He didn't like it but he understood it. Hull was always worried that I was going to hurt him, and I liked it that way.

Blackhawks coach Mike Keenan knew how ruthless I could be, and he would hint strongly when he wanted me to go after someone. He wouldn't tell me directly to go after an opponent, but he would describe in detail how badly the player was hurting us.

In one regular season game that player was Messier, but I resisted. You go to war when it is time to go to war. You don't go to war in a regular season game.

Once, Hullie thought that Keenan wanted me (or one of my teammates) to go after him. When we lined up for the opening faceoff, Hullie asked, "You aren't going to listen to that asshole, are you?"

Sometimes my reputation was enough to knock someone off his game without me even touching him. Other times action was required.

During the 1991 Canada Cup, I was playing for the American team against the Czech Republic. Tomas Jelinek took a run at Brian Leetch and injured Leetch's shoulder. Then, Jelinek nicked Kevin Hatcher with a high stick. On the bench, guys were talking about going after Jelinek. I said I would take care of it. And I did.

Jelinek, who played briefly with the Ottawa Senators, was leaving for a change when I jumped on the ice. I cross-checked him in the mouth and watched his front teeth fly over my shoulder.

He just stood there screaming my name. I went right back to the bench.

My U.S. teammate Mike Modano saw what happened and he located Jelinek's teeth, stickhandled them, and then placed them carefully on the dasher with the blade of his stick. All of the guys on the bench were laughing.

Later that night, I was riding the elevator at our hotel when the door opened and there stood Jelinek. He had just returned from the hospital and his face was all stitched up. A row of his teeth was missing.

Thank heavens I happened to be with Hatcher, who was about 6'5". Jelinek didn't start any trouble.

BY PLAYING THE WAY I did, I accepted the fact that I would be on a lot of hit lists around the league. Much of the time, I got what I deserved.

That might have been the case in 1985 when Boston's Terry O'Reilly caught me with a check that forced me to have knee surgery. On the play, I was coming around the back of the net and Geoff Courtnall pushed me, knocking me off balance. At the same time, O'Reilly cut me off from the other side. Right when he went to hit me, he dropped down and his hips drove right into my knee. No penalty was called on the play.

The Canadiens and the Bruins were fierce rivals at the time, and O'Reilly and I had crossed paths before. As a result, I have always suspected that hit was no accident. In fact, I probably had it coming.

One of his teammates later told me that O'Reilly said hurting me "was better than winning the Stanley Cup."

"How would he know?" I asked. "He never won a Stanley Cup."

I'm not sure if the guy was joking or not, but it seemed like something O'Reilly might say.

I am buddies with Keith Tkachuk, my former Team USA teammate and a great NHL player, but he told ESPN.com that, despite the bond we had after playing together for our country, I had "a face you wanted to punch."

That probably had something to do with the fact that I once put him in a choke hold during a pileup in an important game. When his feet stopped kicking, I let him go, tapped him on the chest, and said, "Got you."

In the penalty box, he claimed that I could've killed him. But that's crazy—it wasn't even a playoff game.

As a general rule, I only became totally ruthless during the postseason. But there were other trigger points that would set me off. For example, I didn't like showboating, and I didn't like guys padding their statistics at my team's expense.

I went after Luc Robitaille of the Los Angeles Kings once because he had two goals and I knew all he was thinking about was getting his hat trick. He came back after me, and I laughed right in his face. I threw a couple of punches before the linesmen stepped in and stopped me from destroying him.

It was common in those days for linesmen to step in when a non-fighter like Robitaille was involved in a scrap. That always bothered me, because when I was getting beat up in a fight, nobody ever stepped in and saved me. Honestly, I think the linesmen enjoyed watching me get pummeled because I was a pain in their ass.

At the time, Robitaille and I had the same agent, Pat Brisson, and Pat was mad at me because he wanted Luc to get his hat trick. But I was very pleased that I took Robitaille off the ice. He is about the nicest guy in the world but he always made it look easy on the ice. He would shoot the puck, and the puck would go in the net. It was that simple for him. And it bothered me when guys made the game look simple, because it wasn't for me.

I've always had crazy strength for someone my size. I only weighed 187 pounds, but my slap shot was timed at 101 miles per hour. My dad taught me how to arm wrestle, and no one my size has ever defeated me. I've always half-believed in that Greek warrior mystique.

You have to be ruthless to stay on top in this game, and I know how to thrive when the line between acceptable and unacceptable is blurred. That is true on and off the ice.

My former Montreal Canadiens teammate Larry Robinson once called me a "junkyard dog" who would do anything to win.

"He'll do whatever it takes to defend his end of the ice," Robinson said. "He'll break your ankle with a slash or put his stick right through you if he has to."

That's all true.

Some players talk about doing whatever it takes to win. I actually did whatever it took to win. That certainly played a role in helping me become a Hall of Fame player in 2013.

Included in the pages of this book is the story of how I wound up standing at that podium. I hope you enjoy the trip as much as I did.

MADE IN AMERICA

1

More Beaches, Less Ice

probably inherited my work ethic from my father, who I think came up with a new way to earn money every single day of his life.

Kosta "Gus" Chelios started out driving a truck in Chicago and ended up owning a handful of different restaurants. No one sought the American dream more aggressively than my father. When he was a 15-year-old kid living in Greece, he lied about his age to enlist in the country's air force. He immediately became a mechanic, working on British-made Spitfires. He moved to America in 1951 hoping to raise a family and have a better life than he would have in Greece. My dad and mother, Susan, had five kids. I was the oldest, and I had three sisters— Gigi, Penny, and Elena—and one brother, Steve.

When I was 10, my dad came home one day and announced we were all moving to Australia. He had a buddy who owned farms down there and was supplying U.S. troops in Vietnam with dairy and meat products. My dad was buying into the business.

Just like that, we packed up our life into 48 trunks and headed off to a new world.

Since my dad wanted to bring his car, we couldn't fly. We drove from Chicago to San Francisco, and then boarded a

42,000-ton cruise ship named the *Oriana* that took us to Fiji, then New Zealand, and finally Sydney, Australia. The boat trip lasted 20 glorious days.

The *Oriana* was almost three football fields long, and I explored every inch of that ship. It was like being on an adventure. One day, I ascended all the way up to the captain's bridge before anyone thought to ask me where I was going.

Being on that ship was like spending three weeks at summer camp. This ship was designed for people on vacation so they had events planned for children every day.

When we arrived in Australia, I became very popular with the U.S. servicemen on leave from Vietnam because I was the only person in Australia who owned an American football.

I played with those soldiers every day, and ended up giving them the football to take back to Vietnam.

Unfortunately for our family's finances, a month after we arrived, it was clear the Vietnam War was ending and my dad was left holding the bag on his business venture.

When he informed my mother that we had to pack up and travel home by boat, she informed him that she had her own plan. She was going to fly home with the children, and my father could travel home on the ship with our 48 trunks and his beloved car.

The saving grace was that my father had structured the deal on our house in Chicago so that we had a window during which we could cancel the contract. So, after we lived in a hotel for a good long while waiting for the people in our house to move out, we moved back into our house on 101st Street.

During the short time we were in Sydney, my father noticed that Australia had no fast food restaurants. After we returned to Chicago, he pursued the McDonald's franchise rights in Australia. In hindsight, he says he had the wrong partners and someone else ended up with the Australian McDonald's.

The stock price for those first 60 McDonald's franchises in the 1970s was trading at $310 per share, my dad remembers. He said if he had just registered the McDonald's name in Australia, he would have made a nice profit. That would have only cost him $350.

"I blew that one," he said.

MY WILD SIDE WAS also probably inherited from my father. Everyone loved my dad. He knew everybody. He was the guy on the street who organized the block parties. He was always in the middle of every event. But he also had an edge to him. He was rough. He was the kind of man who would yell at officials during games, and get into arguments and fights with other parents. If he got pulled over by the police for a driving infraction, it would end up with a confrontation.

We lived on the south side of Chicago, in Evergreen Park, and that alone toughened me up. I did not have a normal childhood.

People from all walks of life would end up at our house. Poker games would sometimes last three days. Sandwiches made by my mother kept the players going through the night.

In between working at our family's restaurants, my mother ended up getting a good job as a waitress in a nightclub. She made enough money to allow my dad to stay home and take care of his children. He put us all in sports leagues and insisted we work hard at whatever we did.

I remember playing Pee Wee hockey and my dad quizzing me about why I hadn't played as well as I had been playing. I had no good answer.

"Don't you like hockey?" he asked. "If you don't like it, let me know right now because it is very expensive."

"Yes, I like hockey," I said. "I like it very much."

"Then I'm going to be with you all of the time, telling you not the good things you do, but rather the bad things you do."

To my dad, sports participation was about working hard. His dream was that my participation in sports would lead to a college scholarship. But that wasn't my dream at that age. I just loved playing.

Growing up in Chicago, I had as much success as a baseball player as I did as a hockey player. I was a Greg Maddux–style control pitcher, able to throw the ball where I wanted with consistency. Using a fastball and a slow curve, I could paint the corners and move the ball around to keep the hitters off balance.

My pitching rival in Evergreen Park was Donn Pall, who ended up pitching 10 years in the major leagues for the Chicago White Sox, Philadelphia Phillies, New York Yankees, Chicago Cubs, and finally the Florida Marlins. He is also remembered for giving up Mark McGwire's 57th home run in 1998, the one that broke Hack Wilson's National League record.

Although we played on different teams during the season, we were supposed to be on the same Evergreen Park team at the state tournament. But Pall's dad was the manager of the team and he decided to play me in right field. When my dad showed up at the game and saw me out there, he pulled me off the team. That was the end of my baseball career.

All of my youth hockey days in Chicago were spent as an undersized center, not a defenseman. I was a scorer. I knew where to be and where to go to be successful. I played for the St. Jude Knights and the Chicago Jesters.

My dad always said that my brother, Steve, six years younger than me, was a better player than I was. But Steve wasn't disciplined enough and didn't respect his coaches enough to take advantage of his talent. He was a defenseman and played major junior hockey in the Quebec Major Junior Hockey League, the Ontario Hockey League, and the Western Hockey League, and then bounced around in the minor leagues until about 2000. He even played briefly in Holland.

Throughout my childhood I worked for my father in the restaurant business. I did what needed to be done: I cleared the tables, washed dishes, and stacked, cut, or carried whatever needed to be stacked, cut, or carried.

When my father owned the Blue Note on Halsted, I was the coat check boy. I remember a guy named Guitar Red playing there. I liked his sound. I also worked in the Grecian Mist near Bridgeview, as well as a few other places. Kids who grew up in my era knew about cartoons and sports heroes. I knew about restaurants.

It wasn't easy working for my dad. A few pots, pans, and dishes were thrown my way when I wasn't doing a task the way he wanted it done.

"There are three doors in the restaurant," he once told me, "and when you see me mad, you should probably go out one of them and then come back later and I will be better."

I was a quiet kid growing up who played the piano, clarinet, cornet, and saxophone. I only played the clarinet because my father made me. It was a Greek thing. When I was in eighth grade, I played clarinet in the Central High School band. I was also playing hockey, and when there was a conflict, I picked up a stick, not a clarinet.

One weekend, the band competed in a state competition and I was playing in a hockey tournament. When I came back to school on Monday, the teacher called me out in front of the entire band.

"Someone thought it was more important to play hockey than to be with his classmates," the teacher said.

I was in the last row, because that's where the weakest musicians sat. I stared at my teacher for a second or two, then rose from my seat and walked out. I never played the clarinet again. That was the end of my musical career. My dad wanted to kill that guy. I was just thankful to be done with band.

When a family friend paid my way to Mount Carmel High School, a Catholic school in Chicago, I was able to play baseball and hockey for a couple of years. I played on the junior varsity hockey team, but I had one memorable varsity goal. When one of our top centers was suspended for the championship game, I was promoted to play against Brother Rice. Given the opportunity to play on a scoring line, I scored both goals in a 2–1 victory. My second goal came with eight seconds to go in the game.

Immediately after the game, a couple of my teammates and I jumped in a car and drove to Waukegan to play for the St. Jude Knights in the state championship game. We missed one period, but we ended up winning the game.

It was the only great day of my high school career. The Chelios family was on the move again.

BY THE FOLLOWING FALL, my dad had lost his restaurant and decided to move us to San Diego with the hope of opening another establishment.

He went to visit a friend there, and then called my mother and said, "It's a paradise."

The restaurant he opened in San Diego did turn out to be his best one. When he sold it, he made a couple hundred thousand dollars.

Going to California was not a strategic move based on furthering my hockey career. I played midget hockey out there, but the competition wasn't good. We were coached by John Miszuk, a former professional player who had toiled for several teams in the NHL and for the Baltimore Blades, Michigan Stags, and Calgary Cowboys in the World Hockey Association.

Our midget team didn't even have a nickname. We were called "San Diego" and had a Jack in the Box logo on our jerseys.

Because the competition was lacking, a couple of my teammates and I started traveling three times each week to play for a team in the Los Angeles area. Occasionally, we would travel to Phoenix or Seattle for tournaments.

While other top players in my age group were playing for high-level programs, I was playing for an L.A. team that primarily played the same opponent over and over. We won the state championship one season because we had no other team in our category.

In the late 1970s, Americans had a minimal presence in the NHL. It was still primarily a league led by Canadians. Colleges also looked to Canada first for talent, and when NHL scouts and college recruiters did look at American players, they certainly weren't looking in San Diego.

You looked for vacation homes in San Diego. You didn't look for hockey players.

The chance of my ending up playing college hockey or making it to the NHL probably would have been calculated as next to nonexistent.

But none of that mattered to me at that time; I had no clue about the lack of Americans in the NHL, nor did I give any thought to my chances of being a college or professional player. I didn't know anything about Canadian junior hockey. I wasn't on USA Hockey's radar when I moved to San Diego, and USA Hockey wasn't on my radar.

If you asked a 16- or 17-year-old Chris Chelios what he thought he would do with his life, he probably would have said "get a business degree from a college in San Diego."

I did love playing hockey, and I was hoping to find a way to continue playing. But at that time of my life I was spending more time on the beach than on the ice. We surfed almost every day. When I wasn't working at my dad's restaurant, I was in the water as much as possible.

I'm sure my parents believed San Diego would be a safer place than Chicago for my siblings and me to grow up, but that turned out to be a false assumption. Five students were killed while I was at Mira Mesa High School. Another student was stabbed at a beach party but survived. Even our straight-laced student president was involved in a knife fight.

A few police cars would show up after school each day and tell us to go right home.

I did some crazy stuff when I was living in San Diego, including jumping off one of the cliffs at La Jolla known as The Clam. In 1994, San Diego officials banned cliff jumping into the Pacific

Ocean because of the danger, but when I was there it was a rite of passage.

There are many different kinds of jumps at The Clam. There are a couple of easy ones, but most of them will make your stomach drop. The easiest jump is seven feet from the water and the hardest jump is from Dead Man's Cliff, 107 feet above the ocean. You are thinking that crazy Chelios probably jumped from that one, but you would be wrong. I made the jumps that are about 35 or 40 feet above the water.

The jumps have inviting names like Thread the Needle, The Wall, The Pass, The Point, The Pedestal, The Bear Claw, and The Double Bear Claw. But those of us who lived in the area understood that despite the fun names, the jumps themselves were quite dangerous.

During the daylight hours, most of the jumps are relatively easy. At night, it's a different story. You have to stand at the cliff's edge and use the moonlight to judge the swells on each jump. Depending on the swells, the water you're jumping into could be anywhere from 10 feet to 30 feet.

On a night jump, my friend James O'Connell struck rocks on the way down and cut his back severely. We spent the night in the emergency room. Many people have been injured, and a couple of jumpers have been killed.

The other problem at night was that people were usually drinking and not thinking.

I like to believe that I was always careful when I jumped. I would dive or do flips off the cliffs during the day but at night I would only jump.

None of my friends ever made the leap off Dead Man's Cliff, but I saw other people do it. They would wear tennis shoes to protect their feet. I saw crazy people ride bicycles off that cliff. I'm sure they were under the influence when they did that.

I think more people injured themselves climbing up the cliff than were injured jumping off. If you fell climbing back up, you were likely to hit your head on rocks on the way down. When you were jumping off the cliffs, at least you were pushing yourself away from the rocks.

As much as I wanted to have fun out there, I was smart enough to avoid taking unnecessary risks.

Cliff jumping wasn't my only dangerous endeavor in San Diego. O'Connell was a motocross rider, and one time, when his bike's engine was shot, we pushed it to the top of the mountain, into the foothills. It took us two hours to get up there. Then O'Connell climbed on the front of the bike, I climbed on the back, and we rode it down the hill as fast as we could go on a full coast.

It was the wildest 15 minutes I've ever experienced.

We were hurtling down the hill as though we were rocket propelled. We made jump after jump. On the biggest one, I believe we were airborne for five or six seconds. Thankfully we never crashed, because we would have been seriously injured. It was certainly not the brightest decision in my life.

Although I survived that death-defying run, I was hurt on another day when I rode down on my own bike. I was wearing a helmet and all of the protective gear I was supposed to be wearing, but while making a jump, my foot slipped off and I ripped my shin open. The cut looked as wide as the Grand Canyon. Unfortunately, my family had no health insurance. So I just bandaged it and went on with my life. That's probably why I have such an ugly scar there today.

IT SEEMED AS THOUGH my luck was changing for the better when U.S. International University at San Diego started a NCAA college hockey program in 1979. After my high school gradua-tion, I enrolled there with the idea of trying out for the team as a walk-on.

Maynard Howe was the first coach, and I actually played against him and his brother in the men's senior league.

The problem was that Canada had hundreds of junior players or former junior players who were excited about the possibility of leaving the frozen north to play hockey in a city where the beach was only minutes away. These players looked at the USIU program as their chance to hit a daily double—they could play hockey and then hit the beaches and party.

I couldn't blame those guys for being interested—I could have told them it made for a pretty sweet life.

Most of the players trying out were older and more experi-enced than I was. I was a 5'10", 155-pound center competing against players who were two, three, or four years older. They were more physically mature.

Predictably, I got cut. In hindsight, I probably didn't deserve to make the team. It looked as if my hockey career was over before it truly began.

One day, I came into the restaurant late for the dinner rush, and my dad erupted. He pulled down a rack of bread on top of me. I walked out of the restaurant and vowed that I would never work for my father again. It was a vow that I kept.

But at that moment I needed a plan, and the plan was pre-sented to me a short time later at La Jolla Shores Beach.

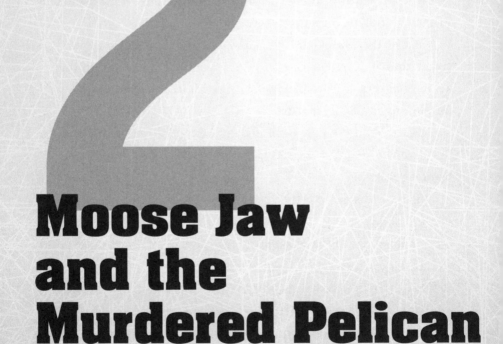

2

Moose Jaw
and the
Murdered Pelican

My entire NHL career was based on a lie I told during a 30-second telephone conversation in 1979.

On La Jolla Shores Beach, near San Diego, I bumped into Bobby Parker, one of the guys who had tried out with me for the local college team. He had made the squad, but decided he didn't like the school or the caliber of hockey being played. He was also homesick. He had decided he wanted to return to his Canadian hometown of Moose Jaw, Saskatchewan, to play Tier II junior hockey. He suggested I call his coach, Larry Billows, and ask for a tryout.

The call to Billows changed my life forever. I had never heard of him before Parker mentioned his name. Billows was a former minor league player who had scored 31 goals in 1968–69 playing for the Amarillo Wranglers in the now-defunct Central Hockey League and 30 goals for the Long Island Ducks of the equally dead Eastern League in 1972–73. When we talked, Billows was the new 33-year-old coach of the Moose Jaw Canucks of the Saskatchewan Junior Hockey League.

Billows needed players, and Parker had told him I could skate. Billows had never seen me play.

"What position do you play?" Billows said.

"What positions do you need?" I asked.

43

"I need a D man," he said.

"Good," I said, "because I play defense."

That was a lie. When those words tumbled out of my mouth, I had never played a single minute of defense in my life. I had been a forward throughout my youth career in Chicago and San Diego. But I felt as if I had nothing to lose if I said I could play defense.

My opportunity almost slipped away because I was broke and needed the Canucks to pay for my flight to Saskatchewan. Billows initially refused that request.

The year before, I had paid for my own flight to Montreal to attend a tryout for a team in Hawkesbury, Ontario, a city near the Quebec/Ontario provincial border. I was cut after playing one game, so I traveled down for another tryout in Chatham, Ontario. Again, I was cut. Then there was another tryout near Windsor. Same result.

After a couple of weeks of starring in the Chelios Traveling Tryout Show, I found myself sitting alone in Detroit's bus depot without a dime in my pocket. The ticket clerk was unmoved by my story, or by the oath I swore to send him the money for a ticket as soon as I arrived in San Diego.

His policy was firm: no money, no ticket.

However, my tale of woe did move two brothers with rotted-out teeth who were listening intently as I explained my plight at the ticket window. They loaned me the money to return home.

They were two funny guys who told me their life story as we rolled across the countryside. They claimed their family owned the farm near Gillsburg, Mississippi, that had been the site of the plane crash that killed members of the band Lynyrd Skynyrd in 1977. They talked nonstop from Detroit to Utah, where they finally exited the bus. I was never so glad to get home as I was after that trip. (I did send the brothers their money.)

So, there was no way I was going through a repeat of that situation and paying my own way up to Moose Jaw. That's why when Billows said he would give me a tryout, I said I needed airfare.

"Sorry, I can't help you," he said.

At that moment, it seemed as if my adult hockey career might be restricted to the California beer leagues. But the Canucks must have lost their next game because Billows called back four days later and said he was willing to pay for my flight. Off I went to a foreign country to play a foreign position.

PARKER STARTED LAUGHING WHEN he read in the Moose Jaw newspaper that Billows was bringing in an American defenseman to help the team. Parker knew that I had never played defense in my life, but he didn't say a word to the coach.

Playing defense turned out not to be as difficult as I had imagined it would be. To be honest, I didn't have to skate backward all that often. I would carry the puck on offense, and then angle guys off the puck when our opponents came back in our direction. It was like I was playing the rover position from 1910-era hockey.

Parker and I have remained friends for years, and he has often told me that he was surprised that I didn't look out of place on the blue line. But my strength was my skating, and I used it effectively to create plays and get myself out of trouble.

I scored on my first shift in my new league and had a good game overall. So I was surprised when Billows came up to me afterward and said, "If you are going to play in this league, you are going to have to fight."

"I've never had a fight on the ice in my life," I said.

"You are going to have to learn," Billows said.

I recall doing okay in my first fight, but my second fight was against Garth Butcher and he kicked the shit out of me. He was only 15 and I was 18 when that happened. Butcher was a big, beefy, ornery defenseman who ended up playing 14 seasons in the NHL. Later in the season, I fought Butcher again and did much better.

Just as I did with other aspects of hockey, I worked at making myself a better fighter. I believed boxers had the best ideas on how to train, so I emulated their training routines as much as I could. I ran all of the time and I worked with the heavy bag. The more I worked on the heavy bag, the longer I could last in my on-ice fights. When I started out, I was a right-hand-dominant fighter, but by working at it I developed a decent left.

The more challenging issue was dealing with the fact that I was the only American playing in a Canadian league, long before the Canadians learned to accept the fact that Americans could play hockey. I was a tan kid from California with long black hair. Opponents must have believed I looked like a Native American because they stuck me with the nickname "Squaw-bait."

Other guys called me "Yankee," and the general impression I had was that most players in this league wanted the American kid to go home.

When it was reported that Mike Eruzione and the American boys won the Olympic gold medal in Lake Placid in 1980, we were on a team bus and some of my teammates turned off the broadcast so I couldn't listen to it. Back then, the Canadians didn't much like it when Americans had success in their sport. I was shaved twice in hazing rituals because of that Lake Placid triumph.

Despite those incidents, most of the razzing from my team-mates was light-hearted, and some of the guys on that team looked after me.

And, as it turned out, I wasn't the only American in the league. We were playing Regina in my second season, and I was surprised to look across the ice and see John Thompson. I had played Midget hockey with Thompson in San Diego and somehow he ended up in the SJHL. To this day, I still don't know how Thompson ended up playing for Regina.

IN MY TWO YEARS in the Saskatchewan League, I amassed 295 penalty minutes in 108 games. I was ninth in the league in penalty minutes in my first season, and fifth in the second season. A chunk of those PIMs resulted from standing up for myself as an American on foreign soil.

Parker and I were defensive partners, and by our second season together we were among the league's most dominant per-formers. In 1980–81, Parker was third in the SJHL scoring race with 100 points and I was eighth with 87 points. We also ranked second and fifth in penalty minutes; Parker totaled 216 and I had 175.

The Canucks were a good team in the two seasons I was there, and I was a big part of the team's success. We were 44–15–1 my first season and 46–14–0 in my second season. We had a good team and it was a good league.

We played in the now-demolished Moose Jaw Civic Centre Arena, nicknamed the "Crushed Can" because of its unique sunken roof. Back when I played there, smoking was still allowed in the building and there was a cloud of smoke that hung about

10 to 15 feet above the ice. When the puck would go airborne it would disappear into the cloud.

When you factor in the Zamboni exhaust, we were probably breathing more than our fair share of carcinogens.

But that barn in Moose Jaw was a great place to play, and it was always packed with close to 3,000 paying customers. When fans would yell from the upper reaches of the arena, it was as if the sound was funneled directly down to the ice. You could hear every word uttered in the stands.

The SJHL was a good option for those players who had not made up their mind whether they were going to play college hockey or major junior hockey. Once you committed to major junior, you surrendered your college eligibility. If you played Junior B, you could still play college hockey. It was a league for players looking for college scholarships.

In the two seasons I was in the SJHL, the future NHL players included Butcher, James Patrick, Gord Sherven, Lane Lambert, and Dave Tippett, who now coaches the Phoenix Coyotes. Terry Simpson was coaching the SJHL team in Prince Albert that beat us both seasons for the league championships. He went on to coach with several teams in the NHL.

The only identifiable NHL prospect we had on our team was Jim Archibald, who was drafted in the seventh round by the Minnesota North Stars after scoring 46 goals in 52 games for us in my second season with the Canucks. He ended up playing college hockey at North Dakota and then a smattering of games for the North Stars.

Archibald was a colorful character. I used to go hunting with him and his seven brothers-in-law. My last hunting trip with him was the one I remember most, because I thought he was going to kill me.

He took me to this abandoned farmhouse that was no bigger than a bedroom. But it had a crawl space under the house, with a small doorway and a set of stairs leading down to it. Archibald crawled down with a firearm and heard a hissing noise coming from a dark corner.

"There's a bunch of raccoons down here," Archibald said. "Come and hold the flashlight for me."

Being the dummy that I was at the time, I crawled down there with him and manned the flashlight. I hadn't been down there long before I sensed something moving on my left. I swept the light 90 degrees in that direction and spied a huge porcupine charging us.

I dropped the flashlight and fled up the opening, leaving Archibald screaming behind me.

"Get back down here and hold the flashlight!" Archibald yelled as he fired away.

"No way!" I said.

Within about 20 seconds, Archibald had killed five raccoons and a porcupine. It was the last time I ever went hunting with him. I don't think I've ever gone near a gun again since that night.

I should have known better than to go hunting with him because Parker had a similar experience a couple of months before.

Parker and Archibald had gone hunting for geese and didn't have any luck. Apparently, Archibald was bound and determined to kill something, because Parker said he shot an owl off a fence post and then blasted a frog with a shotgun. Archibald also spotted an ant hill and blew it to smithereens.

Just when Parker thought he had seen it all, they walked by the local dam, where Archibald spotted a pelican on the water.

The bird took flight about 25 feet from Archibald and he raised his gun and blew it away.

That was the last straw for Parker. He wouldn't have anything to do with Archibald again.

"It was totally senseless," Parker recalled.

Archibald had an edge when he played, as well. We all saw him lose control during a line brawl with the Regina Pat Blues that escalated into a bench-clearing brawl. Because they were the Tier II team for the Regina Pats major junior team, the Regina Pat Blues always carried several younger players on their team. I'm talking 15-, 16-, and 17-year-olds.

During the brawl, Archibald ended up opposite a 16-year-old and was just brutalizing him. He had him in the bench and just wouldn't quit. Finally, some of our guys stepped in and pulled Archibald off the kid.

Archibald had a short fuse, and when he snapped, some opponent was going to pay the price. We were beating the Melville Millionaires one time by more than 10 goals in the third period. The Millionaires goalie came out to freeze the puck and Archibald skated up to him and drove both of his knees into the poor kid's head.

Archibald was a wild beast on the ice. He was unpredictable and could be pretty scary.

I might have been willing to do anything to win, but even I had limits.

WHEN I WAS PLAYING in Moose Jaw, it almost seemed as if I was playing professional hockey, because I always had a little money in my pocket.

I received $200 per month to cover my expenses, plus the team found me a job at the local lumber yard. Because I was an American and couldn't legally work without fighting through a bunch of international red tape, the folks there just paid me in cash.

Two other teammates, Wayne Wagner and George Paterson, worked with me. We unloaded boxcars filled with lumber and loaded sheets of drywall onto trucks.

The worst was when a load of coal would arrive. It would take us three days to shovel all of the coal out of the car. We would be blowing soot out of our noses and coughing up black mist for a week. On coal-shoveling days, we earned our money.

The Canucks didn't usually practice until 4:00 PM because most of the players on the team were either in school or had jobs. I was essentially working full-time, probably bringing in about $200 per week. It seemed as if I had a high-paying job; maybe that's because Dad never gave me a paycheck when I worked for him.

The time I spent in Moose Jaw was one of the most enjoyable periods of my life. I had purchased a piece-of-shit 1966 yellow Volkswagen Beetle from my San Diego buddy Russell Lowell. I paid $400 for the car and then drove it 1,737 miles to Moose Jaw.

My teammates were all laughing when I drove into the arena parking lot because the car was still covered in sand from the San Diego beaches. Plus, my buddies in San Diego had painted a mural of palm trees and the ocean on the driver's side door just to razz me about going off to Canada to play hockey.

The Volkswagen was always a source of humor for my teammates.

One time, it conked out on the east side of town. I called teammate Wendal Jellison and asked him to jump in his 1975 Chevrolet Nova and help me tow it to a mechanic.

"Where's your tow rope?" I asked when he showed up.

"I figured you must have one," he said.

When it was clear that we were both knuckleheads, we hatched a plan. I tied my Beetle to the back of his Nova with a pair of 96-inch hockey skate laces tied together.

I am not making this up. He pulled my car three or four miles across town—over a bridge, on a main road—using our skate laces.

I had plenty of fun in that death trap until it died a noble death on the road to Regina.

The Canucks' team bus wouldn't start when we were scheduled to leave to play a road game. A few of my buddies and their hockey bags piled into my Beetle and we started to drive the 46 miles to Regina. About 20 miles outside of Moose Jaw, the car blew its engine. That's where I left it, parked on the Saskatchewan prairie. I never saw it again. We removed my stereo and hitchhiked to the game.

After the demise of the Beetle, I bought a white 1966 British-made Vauxhall from our goalie, Norm Renwick. I recall that it cost me two or three hundred dollars.

Once, while I was on a college recruiting trip to Madison, Wisconsin, my Moose Jaw teammates Jellison, Parker, Greg Squires, and goalie George Peters borrowed the Vauxhall to make a 90-mile drive southeast to Weyburn, Saskatchewan, because Jellison wanted an acupuncture treatment on his injured shoulder.

The only reason they took my car instead of one of theirs was because I had the best stereo system. My teammates have memories of me tooling around town with my stereo blasting AC/DC or Motörhead or Daredevil. I still have a box in my basement with 10 or 12 cassettes from my Moose Jaw days.

But I would have advised them against taking my car if they had asked, since their cars were far more dependable than mine.

Predictably, my Vauxhall broke down on them just outside of Weymouth.

Squires' dad rescued the group and then gave them a reliable vehicle to make the trip back to Moose Jaw. My car was not rescued.

When I returned from Madison, the guys told me they had abandoned my car as if it was road kill. They didn't figure my car was valuable enough to save.

I didn't see it that way, and I convinced some people to join me on a salvage mission. Needless to say, I was miffed at my teammates for stealing my Vauxhall and then leaving it to die. But I couldn't stay mad for very long. After all, it sounded like something I might have done.

JELLISON AND I WERE billet roommates at the home of Don and Ivy Neff, who lived just a couple of blocks from the arena.

My first three attempts at living with a billet family didn't take. I was young and didn't accept authority very well. The billet families seemed to have a difficult time adjusting to the reality that I wasn't home very often.

However, I liked Ivy and she treated us very well. I kept in touch with her for many years.

My teammates always thought it was odd that I wasn't as fond of sleeping as most teenagers. Most of them liked to sleep until 10:00 or 11:00 AM but I usually left the house by 8:00 AM and, as you might imagine, I stayed out very late. Often I would stop at Pyles Gym in downtown Moose Jaw, where you could work out for a couple of Canadian dollars.

Our captain, Wayne Wagner, looked after me in my first season. He won the scoring title and led the league in penalty minutes. He died of cancer a few years ago, far too young.

For a while I lived with a player named Terry Tattam whose dad, Ralph, had been a minor league goalie. Tattam was a good hockey player; he had 16 goals, 34 points, and 168 penalty minutes in 55 games.

He was a smallish player, about 5'9" and 170 pounds, but he was a good athlete. We had a mall in Moose Jaw, and he was strong enough to walk on his hands from one end of the mall to the other.

Tattam was a truly nice guy, but he could become reckless from time to time. At one point, Terry owned a van that had a short in its electrical system that would cause the headlights to malfunction from time to time. Parker recalls driving down the highway one night and being startled to see a grinning Tattam passing him on the shoulder, driving about 100 mph, with his headlights off.

Tattam and his girlfriend took me in after my billet family kicked me out for throwing a New Year's Eve party at their home without permission.

Unquestionably I did some crazy, even scary, things when I was living with Tattam, like the time I decided to parasail off the back of his truck. I was lucky that I didn't kill myself.

Another time Tattam shot a gun at the dirt and I swear I felt the bullet graze me as it ricocheted off the ground. I remember thinking, *This is nuts.*

With the success I was having in Moose Jaw, I did begin to wonder if I could play college hockey. But college recruiters didn't seem to notice me in my first season, even though I had 12 goals and 32 assists in 54 games.

Still, the Moose Jaw organization seemed pleased to have me, although team officials were quite angry when I used Coach Billows' office phone to call my friends back in California. These were the pre–cell phone days; I don't know how big a bill I ran up, but I'm sure it was hundreds of dollars.

I enjoyed playing for Billows. Most players did. All you need to know about him is that he was a good friend of former NHL coach and minor league legend John Brophy. They were old-school guys who seemed to enjoy when the games got a bit wild. Billows would lose his cool now and then but usually he was only tough on us when he needed to be. I liked that about him.

Billows must have liked me because he gave me a set of keys to the rink, knowing that I liked to go in at odd hours and work on my skating and shooting. Often, I would go out drinking with the boys and then pop into the rink at 1:00 or 2:00 in the morning to shoot pucks. That's how I made up for my lost development time in San Diego.

PLAYING IN THE SASKATCHEWAN League in that era was like living in the movie *Slap Shot* because of all the fighting and the many great characters who were involved with the teams.

The Canucks employed an old trainer named "Bullet" Adams, and you could not have made up a more perfect character to have around a dressing room.

If we weren't playing well, he would slam a hockey stick down on the trainer's table, trying to fire us up. It would just make us giggle, because Bullet was about 5'2". Everyone loved him.

It would be impossible for me to believe that any junior team had more crazy moments than the Moose Jaw Canucks had in my two seasons there.

On one road trip to Saskatoon, the team stayed at the classy, stylish Bessborough Hotel, and it was probably never the same after we left.

Bobby Parker and I bought take-out Chinese food, and we parked the leftovers on an open window sill. When somebody reached for it later in the day, one of the containers tumbled out the window.

When we looked below, we discovered that a man on the street was drenched in Kung Pao chicken and sauce. The food had landed squarely on his head.

Later that night, Archibald decided it was time for the annual rookie initiation. Archibald was the worst guy to be the ringleader of the hazing ritual, because he gave no mercy.

Rookies were stripped, their pubic and chest hairs shaved, and then a marker was used to further defile their bodies. Finally, they were wrapped in hockey tape and placed on an elevator with all of the buttons pushed up to the top floor.

Can you imagine an unsuspecting hotel guest, waiting for an elevator, seeing that sight when the doors opened?

After both the 1979–80 and 1980–81 seasons, some Moose Jaw teammates came back to San Diego with me. In the first summer, I came home with Des Lowe, Kim Shick, and Parker. Nothing better than a road trip with hockey players.

On the second trip, I brought home Brian Russell and Parker. We played Jimi Hendrix's version of "The Star-Spangled Banner" every morning as soon as we got up, just to get the day started right.

Russell and Parker also excessively played the Oak Ridge Boys' greatest hits tape and the Gatlin Brothers' "All the Gold in California." I hated those tapes, and on day four of the trip they mysteriously disappeared.

Parker has always speculated that I threw those tapes out the window while we were driving because I wanted to hear AC/DC.

I'm going to let him continue to speculate.

That trip started with us buying two cases of beer and a cooler in Moose Jaw. We packed our beer on ice, the passengers cracked open one each for the road, and we started our trip. Ten miles outside of Moose Jaw, police officers spotted our drinking and pulled us over. I was tagged with a ticket for having open beers in the car. Even worse, the officers confiscated all of our beer. Of course, we pulled into the next town and started the process over again. Another two cases, another cooler, more ice.

On that trip, we ended up going to Jack Murphy Stadium to watch the San Diego Padres play, and a couple of guys beat up Russell and me in the parking lot for parking our vehicle too close to their car.

We had lost Parker somehow, and as he was trying to jump the fence to get back in, a security guard fired a warning shot over his head.

"We usually shoot first and ask questions later when it comes to trespassers," the guard told Parker as he escorted him out of the gate.

It was on that same trip that I took my teammates to The Clam for some cliff jumping into the ocean. We were jumping from about 30 to 40 feet, and Parker ended up scraping his feet on the bottom a couple of times. The guys were more concerned about climbing up on the barnacle-covered rocks than they were making the leap into the ocean.

We also went to Disneyland, and some girls heard the accents of the Canadian-born players and thought we were the Bay City Rollers. It was a comical scene as these girls started freaking out.

At one point, we were driving down the highway when a car ended up doing a 360-degree spin in front of us. He just missed us but he had no idea whether he hit us or not. By then, I knew drunk driving when I saw it.

"Let's go after him and get some money," I said.

We chased him to the beach and waited for him to leave his car. We rifled through it and found his identification with an address.

Later we showed up at his house and convinced him that he had hit us. There was an old dent in the car that we passed off as fresh damage.

We told him we were going to call the police unless he wanted to settle this without involving them. He gave us $700 and we called it even. And we had a very good week living on that money.

We also went to Tijuana, Mexico, just south of San Diego. One of the guys purchased two illegal switchblades and carefully hid them in the car before we crossed back into the U.S. It looked like a routine crossing until the customs agent asked, "Did you buy any firecrackers, guns, or weapons of any kind?"

My 12-year-old brother, Steve, blurted out, "I bought some firecrackers."

None of us had any idea he had bought firecrackers. That prompted a search of our car. We all stood by the curb waiting for them to find the switchblades, but they never did. We had dodged a big problem.

What Parker remembers about that trip was playing backgammon against my father. I told him that my dad was an excellent player, but he didn't believe me after he won his first game.

He did believe me after my dad won the next dozen games.

IF I HAVE ANY regrets about my Moose Jaw career, it was our inability to defeat our Prince Albert rivals in the postseason. I had a rivalry going with James Patrick, who was Prince Albert's top defenseman. That was the same Patrick that would play 1,280 games in the NHL.

Prince Albert had more pro-caliber players than we did. But we took them to seven games in the playoffs both years I was there.

I remember the second Game 7 against Prince Albert better than the first, because we had the lead in that game before they came back to beat us.

We won the first game of the series in Prince Albert, and then lost the second game. As we were traveling back to Moose Jaw on the team bus, Archibald stood up and walked up and down the aisles trying to fire everyone up.

He was carrying on as if we had already won the series, because he felt we would surely win our games on home ice. He talked about how we would raise the trophy.

Then we lost Game 3 by a 7–0 count.

We came back and won Game 4 in overtime, then split the next two games to set up a Game 7.

We were up 2–1 and then Patrick, of all people, scored for Prince Albert to tie it.

With 10 minutes remaining in regulation, Parker had a breakaway. Unfortunately, it was spring, the rink was warm, the ice was bad, and Parker couldn't get anything on the shot. The puck just fluttered toward the net, and Prince Albert goalie Gil Hudon made the save.

A couple of minutes later in a 4-on-4 situation, Prince Albert defenseman Robin Bartell made an unbelievable play to keep a puck in our zone, diving and knocking the puck down out of midair. That was the turning point. He could not make that same play again if he tried 1,000 times. But at that moment, luck conspired against us and Bartell knocked down the puck. He was the Ulf Samuelsson of the Saskatchewan League. Bartell ended up playing 41 NHL games for the Calgary Flames and Vancouver Canucks. He was an abrasive player with some skill.

After making the great play, Bartell went around a defenseman and scored to make it 3–2.

That goal particularly haunts Parker, because it came against a defenseman that hadn't played much in that game. Just before that goal, Parker had asked Billows to use only our top three defensemen and let us try to win it.

We pressed for the tying goal and came close, but eventually gave up an empty-netter.

A kid named Carl Van Camp played for Prince Albert, and in the closing seconds of the game he skated by our bench and swung his stick like a golf club, reminding us that our season was over while the Prince Albert team was going on to compete for a national championship.

We wanted to kill Van Camp.

It was a heartbreaking defeat. No one took it harder than my defensive partner Parker.

His goal had been to play in the NHL. He was a talented player, certainly good enough to play in the college ranks. But in the summer before our second season Parker had started to lose his vision. He didn't tell anyone, but the rink started to look darker to him.

Scouts from Edmonton and Chicago had noticed the impact on his game before he did. He had been considered a pro prospect after his first year, but they told him he was falling off their radar because scouts had noticed a difference in how he played the game.

It was later diagnosed as macular degeneration, a medical condition that results in a loss of vision in the center of one's visual field. Macular degeneration can make it challenging or impossible to recognize faces, although enough peripheral vision remains to allow for other activities. Today, Parker can't drive but he can still work.

But as we played our second season, he didn't know what he had. All he knew was that he was starting to lose his vision. He knew it was getting worse and he wasn't going to be able to continue playing hockey.

When that game was over, Parker knew his career was over. He placed his hand on my shoulder and said, "Chris, you are going to have to do it for both of us, because I'm done."

"Why?" I asked.

He offered no explanation. He says now that he knew I was going to be a player.

"When you leave, don't look back," Parker said. "But when it's all said and done, you make sure you go back and thank all of the people who helped you along the way."

Beer and Badgers

I f you look back on my choice of Wisconsin over North Dakota when it came time to play college hockey, you could say that former NHL player James Patrick made my decision for me.

Not many college recruiters paid much attention to me in my first season in Moose Jaw. But during my second season, all of the major hockey schools started to take interest in the unusual story of the San Diego kid who had become an impact player in the Saskatchewan Junior Hockey League.

Wendal Jellison was a left wing who scored 49 goals in my second season, and he ended up playing college hockey at Bemidji State in Minnesota. He was there when Joel Otto was playing there, just before Otto signed with the Calgary Flames.

Jellison could testify to how heavily I was recruited by colleges and major junior teams in 1980–81. The phone never stopped ringing at our home, and it reached a point where I was far more annoyed than flattered. Many recruiters simply would not take no for an answer.

The Regina Pats of the Western Hockey League was one of the teams that would not quit. If I signed with them, I would no longer be eligible to play college hockey, so that was a nonstarter for me. But they wouldn't give up.

Finally, I couldn't take it anymore. When the Pats called, I said, "I'm ready to sign. Come to Moose Jaw and I will sign the contract."

As soon I hung up the phone, I grabbed my coat and headed toward the door. I had no intention of playing in the WHL. Jellison just shook his head and laughed.

Pats coach Jack Sangster and public relations director Kevin Gallant showed up at my house an hour later. That's pretty impressive given that it is a 45- or 50-minute drive from Regina to Moose Jaw.

Told by Jellison that he did not know where I was or when I would return, Sangster and Gallant decided to wait a while. When it was clear they had been duped, they angrily headed to their car.

Sangster and Gallant told Jellison to tell me that I had made a big mistake. I guess they figured after they told other teams about my disrespectful stunt, those teams would lose interest in me.

Maybe they didn't command the power they thought they did, because my career worked out just fine.

It didn't take me long to narrow my list to Michigan State, Bowling Green, North Dakota, and Wisconsin. I made visits to each of those schools.

The funniest recruiting story came at Wisconsin, where assistant coach Grant Standbrook had informed the veteran Badgers that they had to be very careful where they took me because I was very religious and didn't drink.

Things were a little awkward when I was introduced to the Wisconsin players. I knew immediately that something wasn't right.

Everyone was looking at me as like I was an Amish farmer who had shown up at a meeting of the Hell's Angels.

Finally, Wisconsin forward Brian Mullen broke the silence and asked, "So you don't drink?"

"You have bad information," I said, laughing. "I drink plenty."

Suddenly my recruiting trip became a lot more fun.

As it turned out, my Moose Jaw coach, Larry Billows, had made up the story about me being religious and a non-drinker with the hope that it would make me more attractive to recruiters. He really wanted me to land a scholarship.

My original plan was to attend North Dakota to play for Gino Gasparini. I even signed a national letter of intent. Jim Archibald had already agreed to play there, and I liked Coach Gasparini. Plus, North Dakota was a quality team and only a day's drive from Moose Jaw, so some of my buddies could come down to see me play. It seemed like a good fit for me.

However, the day after Gasparini signed me he also signed Patrick. Patrick was my rival. I didn't want to play alongside him; I wanted to beat him. I didn't want to be his teammate.

I immediately dialed up Gino.

"Having James Patrick at North Dakota wasn't part of the deal," I said.

To his credit, Gasparini respected my feelings and tore up my national letter of intent. Even though he wasn't happy, he was a stand-up guy.

I called up Standbrook and agreed to play for Bob Johnson at Wisconsin. The Badgers had just won the 1981 national championship.

Before I said good-bye to Moose Jaw, I had one last episode of being young and dumb.

My final act of ridiculousness came on the day I was drafted by the Montreal Canadiens. Excited about the possibility of being selected by an NHL team, Gord Flegel, Jim Archibald, and I purchased a couple cases of beer and headed to the river. Our plan was to hang out there and monitor the draft news on the radio. We were each full of hope about our futures in hockey.

Flegel was a smaller forward, but he had netted 51 goals in 60 games that season and had already committed to play at Michigan State on a scholarship. Archibald had scored 46 goals that season and racked up 308 penalty minutes. This was the early 1980s, when hockey games could sometimes resemble a riot on the ice; Archibald's numbers were going to impress somebody.

As it turned out, the Canadiens selected me in the second round, 40th overall, and Archibald was taken 139th by the Minnesota North Stars. It was a bittersweet day because Flegel didn't get drafted. We didn't know what to say to him.

By coincidence, the town was hosting a social that night, which was a city-wide party at a banquet hall. We were told to come because people wanted to congratulate us for being drafted. By then, we had already consumed too much alcohol but that didn't stop us from heading there to drink with our Moose Jaw teammates.

At one point in the evening, I headed off to the bathroom. A pay phone was ringing as I passed. Inexplicably, I paused and answered it. Amazingly, the call was for me. An ex-girlfriend was on the line. She had broken up with me three weeks before, and yet she wanted me to come over.

One of the players at the party was Mike Dreger, who played for the Melville Millionaires and owned a new Chevrolet Monte Carlo. It was a nice ride and he let me borrow it to reunite with my old flame. He may not have realized that in my condition, I should not have been driving, especially in the slick, rainy road conditions that were present that night. I only traveled three blocks before I slammed the Monte Carlo into a pole. I scrambled out of the car and left the scene as quickly as I could, throwing the keys onto the roof of a nearby hotel. I figured I'd deny having driven the car, and I couldn't do that if Mike's keys were jingling in my pocket.

I was soaked and caked in mud when I re-entered the party and explained what had happened.

By the time Dreger and I walked to the scene of the accident, the police had already arrived. We immediately returned to the party to get our stories straight. I went to my ex-girlfriend's house to hide, and Mike told the police that he had been at the party and someone must have stolen his car.

Police were skeptical because they had found our jackets in the car. They made all of the players shake their hair out to see if anyone had glass shards.

The police asked where I was, and my teammates said they had no idea.

The next day I got out of Moose Jaw. Somehow I had dodged major trouble. The car was covered by insurance except for the $300 deductible that I paid.

MY TIME IN MOOSE Jaw had been a great adventure. My career had been launched there, and I met some great people and had a lot of fun. But I was ready to move on to Wisconsin.

My college career was actually delayed four weeks by an injury I suffered while taking part in a freshman initiation night.

A September dinner at the Big 10 Pub ended with some of us downing shot after shot of peppermint schnapps. I remember the count was at 26, but what happened after that is a complete mystery to me.

Somehow I got back to the dormitory and found that it was locked. Too drunk to know any better, I broke the glass with my hand and reached in to open the door.

I was feeling no pain because of all the alcohol I had consumed. But people in the dorm freaked out when they saw me because my hand and arm were a bloody mess. Somewhere in the process I lost consciousness and the paramedics were called. As fate would have it, one of the paramedics who responded was the father of Wisconsin goalie Marc Behrend. He is the one who revived me in the ambulance.

With a blood alcohol level that was off the charts, I was a difficult patient; I attacked the first doctor who tried to help me. And because of the amount of blood I had lost, I didn't get any painkillers when they stitched me up and put a cast on my arm.

I only got a couple of hours of sleep back at the dorm before I was told that Coach Johnson wanted to see me.

Badly hung over, I stumbled to his office. His secretary told me to sit in a chair until he was ready, staring at me with a glance that was equal parts pity and disgust. I was bandaged, bruised, and blue in the face.

When Johnson called me in, I hoped his justice would be swift because I was about to vomit.

"I thought you didn't drink?" he asked, remembering what Coach Billows had claimed.

"I don't usually drink the stuff I did last night," I said.

Badger Bob Johnson lectured me on the evils of drinking, citing examples of athletes whose lives were ruined by alcohol. He was making good points, but it was taking too long and I had to bolt from the chair.

"But I'm not done with you yet!" Badger Bob yelled as I flew out the door.

Once the full story was revealed, he was more angry with the sophomores and juniors who had convinced the freshmen to drain bottles of peppermint schnapps.

In addition to causing me bodily harm, my night of drinking had soured my relationship with the people in charge of my dorm. It put a bull's-eye on my back.

My roommate that first semester was forward and Madison native Tom Ryan. We had a good time together. We hauled in a large refrigerator and then stocked it with beer. That made us very popular. We had a steady stream of customers coming to our room at all hours.

The refrigerator didn't get us in any trouble, but I did eventually get booted from the dorm after I pulled a prank with a fire extinguisher.

One of the campus-sponsored events that year was the showing of movies on the outside wall of the dorm. I came up with the bright idea of blowing foam into the air as people tried to watch the film.

It seemed funnier at the time than it does now.

As soon as I blasted the fire extinguisher, moviegoers started chanting, "Asshole. Asshole." I guess they didn't appreciate my sense of humor.

Being expelled from the dorm turned out to be good fortune because I ended up moving in with Bob and Barb Johnson, who were known for taking in hockey players.

They were no relation to Coach Johnson. As my new landlord liked to say, "I'm the *real* Bob Johnson."

The Johnsons were such a popular billet family that they put a row of five beds above their garage to take in as many players as they could. Bob and Barb were wonderful, tolerant people who let young people behave like young people while still keeping them safe.

THE DECISION TO ATTEND Wisconsin turned out to be crucial because I learned so much from Coach Standbrook and Bruce Driver, who was one of the nation's best defensemen.

Remember, I only had two seasons as a defenseman under my belt, and I played more like a rover when I was in Moose Jaw. I really learned to play defense by listening to Standbrook and watching Driver.

Standbrook taught me all of the little tricks you can do with your stick, such as the "can opener" move, which helps you turn a guy off his path by putting your stick between his legs. That was actually legal back then. He also taught me how to block shots (not that I did that very often) and helped me with my skating. He could watch you for five minutes, then break down your stride and give you pointers on how to make yourself a better skater. He could coach the goaltenders as well. There was nothing he couldn't do. He was a real perfectionist.

Here is how synonymous Standbrook was with hockey; he once had a tryout with the Springfield Indians when Eddie Shore was the coach in 1954–55. When you can drop Eddie Shore's name, you know you've been around the game a long time. I believe a good chunk of Driver's and my success at Wisconsin was all Standbrook's doing. He really taught Driver and me the art of playing defense.

My overall game and conditioning level improved dramatically at Wisconsin. I also undoubtedly developed a reputation as a player who would do anything to win. Opponents considered me ruthless, and I liked it that way. Guys I played against learned quickly that I didn't appreciate players who drew too much attention to themselves.

We had a fierce rivalry with Minnesota, and the Golden Gophers had a very good player named Pat Micheletti. Once he scored a goal against us in Madison that was essentially a tap-in into an empty net. A defenseman shot the puck from the point, and it whizzed past one post and caromed back by the other post and onto Micheletti's stick.

He celebrated that goal as if it had been the clinching goal of a Stanley Cup Final. I didn't appreciate his over-the-top revelry.

"You will pay for that," I said.

He told me where I could stick it, or words to that effect. He could be mouthy.

Later in the game, an opportunity presented itself, and I slashed him as we exited the Wisconsin zone. The officials were looking up ice, and not at us. I struck him on the side of the knee. It turned out to be the right spot. Micheletti said that he couldn't even feel his leg after the slash. He ended up with drop foot, and was out of the lineup for more than three months. He probably didn't deserve it.

I also purposely kneed Minnesota's Bryan "Butsy" Erickson and put him out of the lineup for a while. It was a reaction play but I knew the potential consequences. Erickson, who ended up playing in the NHL, was one of their best players and I just wanted him gone.

It wasn't as if I spent all of my time torturing opponents. I also met my wife, then Tracee Smith, at a fraternity party while I was at Wisconsin. It turned out she was a friend of my teammate Ted Pearson's girlfriend. They negotiated a date for us.

Tracee had no idea that I was a hockey player. I called and asked her to go to the Badgers game that weekend. She said yes, so I told her I would see her after the game. It was a quick conversation.

"This guy is a little rude. He didn't even offer to pick me up before the game," Tracee told her roommate.

Tracee believed that we were both going to the game but that I wasn't planning to sit with her. She didn't figure out I was actually on the ice until 10 minutes into the game.

The Badgers played in Dane County Coliseum, and it was the only college arena at the time that served beer. As a result, the crowds were often crazy and absolutely nuts.

The wildest night had to be on January 30, 1982, when North Dakota and Wisconsin played the famous Water Bottle Game. It was the event that defined the North Dakota–Wisconsin rivalry.

The game included a brawl that spilled into the stands. And which North Dakota player was in the middle of it all? You guessed it—my former porcupine-killing Moose Jaw teammate, Jim Archibald. Other future NHLers on that North Dakota team included goalie Jon Casey, Troy Murray, Craig Ludwig, Rick Zombo, and Phil Sykes.

We were leading 3–0 when one of my teammates, forward John Newberry, squirted North Dakota captain Cary Eades with a water bottle as Eades skated by our bench. It was the second time in the game that had happened, and Eades stopped to confront Newberry. He had pushed his stick up near Newberry's throat when our defenseman Pat Ethier moved down the bench and threw a punch at Eades.

That set off a chain reaction that made the scene at the arena look like a prison riot.

Not surprisingly, Archibald ended up fighting with a fan after his fight with a Wisconsin player spilled into the stands. Ludwig, who later played with me in Montreal, told Eades it was Ethier who had smoked him with the punch. Eades found Pat and those two fought.

It was difficult to keep track of everything that was going on, but just when it appeared things were calming down, Archibald ended up back on the ice and triggered the second round by punching one of our players.

Believe it or not, I was an innocent bystander in all of this. I didn't get paired up with anyone.

When the smoke cleared, Newberry, Ethier, and Steve McKenzie received game misconducts, while Eades, Archibald, and Dan Brennan were tagged with game misconducts for North Dakota. Later, the Western Collegiate Hockey Association added two-game suspensions for Newberry and Eades and five games for Archibald.

North Dakota, unfortunately, got the last laugh after beating us 5–2 in the NCAA championship game in my first year.

You can imagine how irritated I was about losing to Patrick again.

I **LOVED BOB JOHNSON** as a coach. He was enthusiastic and colorful. He was fun to be around. You never knew what he was going to say to you. In the early 1980s, long before players were thinking about nutrition, Badger Bob was.

One day, he saw me eating popcorn in the dressing room.

"A lion doesn't eat popcorn," he said. "Throw it away."

I threw it away.

We all listened to Bob. He was very similar to Scotty Bowman in that regard. You didn't have a conversation with either of those coaches; it was clear that both of those guys knew more about the game than you ever would. You respected what they had to say.

The only guy who would talk back to Johnson was Newberry, who was one of our top scorers. He was a Montreal draft pick like me, but he only ended up playing a handful of games. One time, Johnson did a curfew check and Newberry slammed the door in Johnson's face.

In practice, Johnson would set up his lines to pit the Americans against the Canadians to determine who was going to start the next game. We all wanted to start, and that made the practices highly competitive. We would try to kill each other in those Wednesday or Thursday scrimmages.

Before the game, Bob would tell one of the players to put the marching band music on our stereo and he would march out like he was a band member.

He was a lovable, funny coach. We all had respect for Badger Bob.

After my first season, Johnson left to coach the Calgary Flames. It was a big deal for a college coach to step into the NHL. Colorado College coach Jeff Sauer took over the Badgers. He didn't change a thing, and the players loved that. I liked playing for him. He also kept Standbrook, and that was important to me.

It wasn't easy following Johnson, who had won three NCAA tournaments in 15 years. But Sauer did it better than anyone could have imagined.

We won the national championship in our first season under Sauer, but not without some trying times. We didn't even win the Western Conference Hockey Association championship. We were third, behind Minnesota and North Dakota.

The low point came in early February when we lost 6–3 in Duluth on a night we took 17 penalties.

"We just took the title for penalties," Sauer said after the game. "Now let's stop this chippy stuff and get first in the standings."

Sauer used the word *embarrassed* more than once that night.

At one point, we were 11–8–2 in league play and fourth in the standings. It seemed like we had forgotten how to play hockey. We played sloppy defensively. Sauer was unhappy. Ted Pearson got benched. It could have been any one of us that paid the price, because we had all played poorly.

Sauer told us we needed to change our attitudes, and we did from that point on.

We finished the season on a 13–1–1 run and won the NCAA tournament with a 6–2 win against Harvard in the title game.

Along the way I scored one of the biggest goals of my career to help us win the WCHA playoff championship. The WCHA played two playoff series then, and total goals won the series.

We tied 2–2 in the first game at North Dakota, and then we were behind often in the second game. We had to rally from 2–0 and 3–1 deficits, and we trailed 5–4 going into the closing minutes.

After we pulled goalie Marc Behrend for a sixth attacker, we had pressure on the North Dakota net and I scored on a rebound with 12 seconds left to tie the game.

The puck was just sitting there in the crease and I swung with all of my might. I'm still not sure I ever touched the puck. I might have just driven the goalie, with the puck, over the line. It probably would not have been a goal in today's game, where we have the use of instant replay.

Armed with momentum, we came out strong in overtime. But the game went into a third OT before we believed we had won on a goal by Pearson at 1:02 of the period.

Players were already shaking hands and heading toward the dressing room when the officials notified both teams that they were checking to see if Pearson's stick had a legal curve. Pearson said he checked his stick before overtime, and it was fine. He was happy to hand it over for further inspection.

It was standard to check sticks for illegal curves in that era, and scorers would change sticks going into the third period of close games. You certainly wouldn't risk using an illegal stick in overtime. Plus, you would not expect Pearson to have an illegal stick because he was a solid, dependable, meat-and-potatoes player. He wasn't considered a scorer.

Officials stunned everyone by saying Pearson's stick was illegal and that he was being assessed a two-minute penalty.

Suddenly, North Dakota had both life and momentum. But amazingly, Paul Houck scored a shorthanded goal just 26 seconds later to give us a 6–5 win. Houck's stick was indeed legal.

Pumped up by that win, we downed Minnesota in the WCHA final and that earned us the No. 1 seed in the Western Regional.

In the NCAA tournament, we downed St. Lawrence and then Providence 2–0 in the semifinals and then Harvard 6–2 in the final. Harvard had beaten Minnesota to reach the title game.

Flatley played that game with a bad hip pointer and scored a pair of goals. We were really confident we were going to win that game. Behrand was named the tournament's MVP. He was 17–1–1 that season.

Standbrook liked to write poems to inspire us, and he had one called "The Ring," which was a take on one written by the poet Berton Braley. *Sports Illustrated* even included it in a story written by Jack Falla after we won the championship:

> If you want a ring badly enough, go out and fight for it.
> You've worked day and night for it.
> All season long for it, you've given your time and your peace and your sleep for it.
> And all that you've dreamed and you've schemed is about it.
> If dogged and grim you besiege and beset it,
> You'll get it!

DURING MY SECOND SEASON at Wisconsin, I began to think that I might have a chance to play in the NHL.

After Herb Brooks' team had won the gold medal at Lake Placid in 1980, NHL teams started paying far more attention to American players. The vast majority of our 1980 Olympic team was given a chance to play in the NHL. Adding American-born NHL prospects had become trendy.

There was talk around the NHL that three American-born players—Brian Lawton, Pat LaFontaine, and Tom Barrasso—would be among the first several picks of the NHL draft. No American had ever gone No. 1 before, but Lawton and LaFontaine were in the conversation to be the first pick.

Still, I never really believed I was going to be an NHL player until Team USA general manager Larry Johnson called me around Christmas in 1983 and told me he was willing to guarantee me a 1984 U.S. Olympic roster spot.

USA Hockey was offering guaranteed roster spots to several of the top American players because it was fearful that many of them were going to sign with NHL teams.

That was not true in my case. I was not planning to sign with the Montreal Canadiens after my sophomore season. At the time USA Hockey offered me an Olympic roster spot, my plan was to play four seasons for Wisconsin. I wasn't sitting around dreaming about being an NHL player. I wanted to be the first member of my family to earn a degree. It's possible that Montreal general manager Serge Savard could have changed my mind with a lucrative offer. But turning pro wasn't my main objective.

The Olympic invitation boosted my confidence. That's when I started to think about the possibility of playing in the NHL. I began analyzing the Canadiens' roster and wondering where I might fit in.

The previous summer, the team had traded away two regular defensemen, Rod Langway and Brian Engblom, plus Doug Jarvis and Craig Laughlin, in a multi-player swap with Washington that brought Ryan Walter and Rick Green back to Montreal.

The Canadiens were still among the NHL's best teams, fifth overall in 1982–83, but it looked as if their defense was a reconstruction project. At 31, Larry Robinson was still a dominant NHL star, and Green was an established, noteworthy veteran. But the other defensemen included Gaston Gingras, Gilbert Delorme, Ric Nattress, Craig Ludwig, Robert Picard, Dwight Schofield, Bill Kitchen, and Bill Root, all of whom were either young, unproven, or both. *Maybe*, I thought, *I could fit into that group of younger players.*

In the second half of my sophomore season at Wisconsin, I put considerable effort into training for the Olympics and a possible NHL career. I started to believe I wouldn't be returning to Madison after the Olympics.

At the very least, I figured the Canadiens were going to bring me in to see what I could do.

With that kind of mind-set, I started to put less effort into my classes.

I never earned my degree. It's one of the few regrets I have in life.

4

Only One Miracle Per Customer

My 1984 U.S. Olympic experience was almost derailed during a train trip through Austria days before we were scheduled to arrive in Sarajevo, Yugoslavia.

Coach Lou Vairo's last cut from the U.S. squad was Tim Thomas, a good friend of mine and my former Wisconsin teammate. I was ticked off by that move, believing that politics probably played a role in the decision. In those days, there seemed to be an unwritten mandate that the roster include enough guys from Minnesota and Boston.

Thomas was a Minnesota native, but he played his hockey at Wisconsin. Those kinds of things seemed to matter in national team decisions. Even if politics played no role, I could see no justification for cutting Thomas.

When I looked at our roster, I didn't view Thomas as a guy on the bubble. He was a versatile player, someone who could play both forward and defense. Plus, he was a physical player, and I thought our young team would need some grit and toughness when we played Canada in our first game.

Thomas received the news after we had hammered the Austrian national team, and he was on the train with us before we headed home and then on to the Olympics. Crushed, he went to the bar car to drink and I went with him, in the name of being a good teammate and friend. It doesn't help to blow off steam unless there is a friend with you to reinforce the idea that you have been wronged.

The problem was that U.S. players weren't supposed to be in the bar car, and I was still a U.S. player.

U.S. goalie coach Dave Peterson spied me in there with Thomas. He came in and told me to leave the bar immediately and rejoin my teammates. Tim and I were getting hammered.

During my career, I made it a point never to talk back to coaches. I may have been mouthy on the ice, but I always believed I needed to be respectful at all times to coaches. That's just my personal philosophy.

But I made an exception on this night, and I informed Peterson that I would be along shortly. He usually bullied players but I stood up to him. I didn't curse at him but I was firm.

Clearly I stayed with Thomas longer than I should have. Peterson was furious about the incident, and he wanted me booted off the team. It wasn't the first time he had called for my dismissal. There was another incident in Alaska earlier in the tour involving a night of drinking, and I had heard Peterson believed I should be cut that night, too.

For the second time, after discussing the situation, the coaches decided I should stay.

I've never known for sure who saved me, but I assume Vairo made the final decision. He always treated me as if he liked me.

THE 1984 OLYMPIC EXPERIENCE is not among my all-time favorite hockey memories, mostly because of how poorly we played in Sarajevo.

Because the Americans had won the gold medal in Lake Placid in 1980, we were treated like royalty in 1984 during the Olympic tour. We lived in apartments in Edina, Minnesota, and we were given the use of a new car.

Phil Verchota, a member of the 1980 team, was chosen as the 1984 captain, and he was a solid choice. We called him "Old Man." I've always felt that a team needs veteran leadership, and he was 27 when we arrived in Sarajevo. He wasn't a star player, but I never believed that a captain needed to be a team's best player. He just needs to have a presence in the dressing room, and Phil had that. He was also a nice guy.

We also had another 1980 veteran in John "Bah" Harrington, and he was kind of the anti-Verchota. He had a lot of Herb Brooks in his leadership style. Harrington was harder on the young guys. He was always challenging guys to push their limits.

If you put Verchota and Harrington together, you had every element you want in a leader. We had a good tandem leading us.

The 65-game tour was a long grind, and in every city there was a banquet, and speeches, and more speeches. If it were left up to the players, we would have preferred just to play hockey and do without the pomp and circumstance. But the 1980 team had put the sport on the map, and many communities wanted to have a connection to the 1984 team before it left for Sarajevo.

We even went to the White House and visited President Reagan, who was quite animated and fun. "We had to win to visit the White House," Verchota said.

On paper, we looked like we could be a quality team. Vairo had studied European hockey, and he wanted a team filled with speed.

Our most skilled players—Eddie Olczyk, Pat LaFontaine, and David A. Jensen—were all teenagers. Olczyk, 17, was a fellow Chicago product, and he was expected to be selected early in the 1984 draft. LaFontaine, 19, was picked No. 3 overall by the New York Islanders in the 1983 draft, and Jensen, 18, was still a high school senior but was the fastest skater on our team. The Hartford Whalers had drafted him in the first round.

Defenseman Al Iafrate from the Detroit area was another 17-year-old on our team. Our average age was about 21.

When Iafrate was established as an NHL player, he was considered a flamboyant player. But he was a quiet kid when he played on the 1984 Olympic team. LaFontaine was a very clean-cut kid who didn't drink. I liked him. I remember going bowling with Pat and our girlfriends and having a good time.

Eddie was picked on because he was a pretty confident youngster. He had a high opinion of himself, and older players used to take him to task for that.

Our defense was solid. Tom Hirsch and Gary Haight were probably our two most prominent defensemen. Hirsch played at the University of Minnesota and was a second-round draft pick of the Minnesota North Stars. Haight played for Michigan State.

Using our speed and skill, we blitzed a good Harvard team 11–2, and afterward Harvard coach Bill Cleary told E.M. Swift of *Sports Illustrated*, "We [also] played the 1980 team and this one is quicker."

We were beating some NHL teams, too. After we beat the Washington Capitals, Caps general manager David Poile told *Sports Illustrated*, "They're every bit as good as the 1980 team. We played our whole lineup, and territorially they controlled the play. They're well coached, the system they're playing is similar to the one [Herb] Brooks used, they're quicker than pro teams, and in LaFontaine they have a player who is probably better than any individual who played in 1980."

Given how well we were playing and how much fun we were having, it never occurred to any of us that we were on an impossible mission.

Because of what the 1980 team had accomplished, the expectations for us were three stories above realistic. To make matters worse, we would never be able to replicate the magic of the 1980 Lake Placid moments, no matter what we did.

We were tasked to supply the encore for a once-in-a-lifetime event.

Maybe the most memorable win in the tour came in December, when we downed the Soviet Selects 5–4 on the same Lake Placid ice where Mike Eruzione had scored to down the Soviet Union in 1980.

The entire town of Lake Placid was fired up for the game. People in cars were honking their horns. Everyone had their American flags out. People wanted to relive the 1980 moment. It seemed more like a Stanley Cup Final game than an exhibition game. It was a storybook kind of night.

The game was tied 2–2 at one point, and then Scott Bjugstad stuffed home his own rebound to give us our first lead of the game. Then I knocked in a loose puck to make it a 4–2 game with 5:09 remaining. The crowd erupted.

We believed the game was ours then but that was not the case. The Soviets scored 48 seconds after my goal and then tied it on a goal by their captain, Mikhail Varnakov, with 1:39 remaining.

In the closing minutes, I had noticed that the Soviet defensemen were aggressively pinching up into our zone, trying to make something happen offensively. Instinctually, I yelled for Verchota to look for the home run pass. He had noticed the Soviets creeping up as well.

When the puck was dropped, he was flying up the ice. The puck came back to me, and in an instant I fired a 60-foot pass that hit him in stride as he was churning over the Soviet blue line.

On a breakaway, Verchota skated in and beat the Soviet goalie on the stick side. Bedlam ensued. Fans acted as if we had captured an Olympic medal, and we hadn't won anything.

These were good players, but none of them would be on the Olympic team. We had beaten the Soviet JV team. Still, it was the most exciting win over a JV squad I'd ever experienced.

VAIRO WAS ONLY 38 when he coached us, and he wasn't like most coaches most of us had known. He owned a memorable Brooklyn accent and a penchant for butchering the English language now and then. He liked to play trivia on the bus with his players.

"Hey, Chelios, you went to Wisconsin," he once said to me. "Who is the governor of Wisconsin?"

"Who cares?" was my reply.

Vairo also enjoyed making speeches to his players, and when he would start offering his pearls of wisdom, I would turn on this tape recorder I had.

Later, when we were traveling on the bus, I would replay the speech and everyone would make editorial comments. The boys always enjoyed my Vairo replays.

One of my favorite recordings was of Vairo reaming me out for my conduct during a college game at New Hampshire.

During the first period, I was high-sticked above my eye and the referee missed it. I confronted him and screamed, "How the hell did you miss that?"

His response was to assess me a 10-minute misconduct penalty.

Dr. George Nagobads, a U.S. Hockey Hall of Famer, was our team doctor, and I remember it took him a long time to stitch me up.

When we got back to the dressing room between periods, Vairo told me to remove my gear. I was done for the night. He made me stand on the bench and watch the rest of the game.

When the game was over, he told me he was going to walk me over to the referee so I could apologize. I did approach the referee, but I just told him again that he was incompetent for missing such a blatant penalty.

Knowing I was going to be the target of a Vairo explosion, I clicked on my tape recorder and stuck it into my front pocket.

An angry Vairo did chew me out, and I had every word on tape. Guys on the bus loved that one.

Despite the occasional diatribe, we were not without our share of fun times during the pre-Olympic tour.

Some of my 1984 U.S. Olympic teammates like to tell the story of my coming face-to-face with a seven-foot-tall bear on a team-bonding trip to Alaska.

My U.S. teammate Eddie Lee and I first spotted the bear as we were fishing from a peninsula. We watched him as he poked around, seemingly in search of food. It was like we were in the middle of a National Geographic special observing a bear in his natural habitat. The bear didn't seem all that threatening as we hid in the weeds and watched him meander around for a while.

Then Lee and I both realized simultaneously that the bear had wandered quite close to us, and panic set in. We dropped our fishing poles and started fleeing through the water. A park ranger was nearby, and he was strongly urging us not to run and draw the bear's attention. We responded to that by yelling at him to shoot the bear.

The truth is the bear was never really chasing us. He entered the water only because he was looking to dine on some fish.

It was a comical scene for my teammates, because it looked as if Eddie and I were sprinting through a foot of water trying to escape a large bear. We were scared, but when we finally stopped running we realized we had never been in any true danger. The bear had no interest in the two crazy humans in the water.

Everyone gave us grief for running even though the ranger had said not to. But one of my personal rules is that when I see a bear, I run.

Olczyk said that if I had an encounter with a bear, he might put his money on me. I don't believe I have the same confidence in my bear-fighting skills that Eddie does.

The other memorable event from that trip to Alaska was Tom Barrasso leaving the team to sign with the Buffalo Sabres. He had been the Sabres' first-round pick, No. 5 overall, but he originally agreed to play for the U.S. Olympic team. Although Barrasso was only 18, he was expected to compete against Minnesota-Duluth goalie Bob Mason and my former Wisconsin teammate Marc Behrend for the No. 1 job.

Buffalo owner Seymour Knox flew in and told Vairo that he just wanted to meet Barrasso. He did so—and then flew him back to Buffalo to sign a new contact.

WHEN WE FINALLY ARRIVED in Sarajevo, we were a confident group. Our first game, played before the opening ceremony, was against Canada, a team we had defeated 8–2 the last time we met, in Milwaukee.

The Canadians were not playing that well, having won only two of their last 19 exhibition games.

But Canadian officials received good news before our game when the International Olympic Committee ruled that goalie Mario Gosselin and forward Dan Wood were eligible to play for Canada, even though Gosselin had signed with the Quebec Nordiques and Wood had signed with the St. Louis Blues.

Finland had protested that those players were among 10 spread over five countries who should be expelled for being professionals. But the IOC sided with the Canadians.

Before the first puck was dropped, we started to experience bad breaks. Pat LaFontaine fell ill and was nursing a 103-degree temperature. Then the bus driver taking us to the Zetra Arena got lost and then ensnarled in traffic caused by the Olympic torch run. We showed up to the rink much later than anticipated.

Vairo was a very likable man who treated us well, but he was new to dealing with the big stage as a head coach.

He had the impossible task of trying to follow up what Herb Brooks had done in 1980. I'm sure he thought long and hard about what he should say to us before the game. But it wasn't exactly an inspiring speech.

"Millions of people are going to be watching," he told us. "Don't fuck up."

I will never forget those words as long as I live. I looked at my teammates, and we all had the same expression of disbelief etched on our faces. I think we understood at that moment that we were under enormous pressure to win.

Once the game against Canada started, our luck didn't improve.

In the opening 27 seconds of the game, Carey Wilson, who would go on to play 552 NHL games, took a shot toward the net, and Behrend looked like he was in position to make the save. But my former Wisconsin teammate Pat Flatley tipped the shot past Behrend to give Canada a 1–0 lead.

To say we were stunned would be an understatement.

Things weren't going great for me personally either. Sometime early in that game, I blocked a shot. I couldn't even tell you who fired the puck. It wasn't a dangerous shot but the puck hit me in the wrong spot and cracked a bone in my foot. I kept playing but I knew it was trouble.

I didn't hurt our team, but I no longer had the skating ability to play as aggressively as I needed in order to be a difference-making defenseman. I no longer had the jump.

Wilson ended up with a hat trick in that game and we lost 4–2. Gosselin made 37 saves.

Did the pressure get to us? Were we too nervous? Who knows. But we didn't have it that day, and we let that loss overwhelm us.

I didn't have X-rays taken of my foot until after the tournament. We just operated as if it was a bad bruise. I used a walking cast between games. The biggest problem was that I couldn't take any painkillers because they were on the banned-substance list for Olympic athletes.

I didn't miss any shifts in the tournament but I had to endure a lot of pain to keep playing.

Despite our loss to Canada, we could have salvaged our tournament if we had defeated a talented Czech team in the second game. But we took too many penalties, gave up a pair of power play goals, and lost 4–1. I was in the penalty box for cross-checking when the Czechs netted one of those power play goals.

With two losses against key teams in our first two games, we were essentially out of the medal hunt.

After we tied Norway 3–3, journalists took out their long knives and carved us up.

In hindsight, the only exceptional memory of that first Olympic experience was walking in the opening ceremony. It was spectacular to be surrounded by the greatest athletes in the world. NHL players don't get to walk in the ceremony because they have league games to play.

I know we should have beaten Canada. The Czechs were a better team, but then we almost certainly would have defeated Norway. After all, Norway had lost 16–2 to Finland, a team we had tied.

A lot has been made of Barrasso's decision to leave the U.S. team and its effect on our performance. But it was not a given that he was going to be the starting goalie anyway. Mason and Behrend were in the mix to be our top goalie. I know Barrasso went on that season to win the Calder and Vezina trophies. But at his age, it's impossible to know whether he would have been given the No. 1 job in Sarajevo. Remember, Behrend was older and a two-time NCAA tournament MVP.

Behrend ended up playing for us, and I didn't believe he was at fault for our Sarajevo failures. I thought we were all at fault. We didn't measure up against that level of competition.

WHEN THAT OLYMPIC TOURNAMENT was over, I was already starting to look at the Montreal roster and wondering where I might fit in. I had played two seasons of Tier II Canadian junior hockey, two seasons of college hockey, and one season of U.S. national team hockey. I felt ready to turn pro. I still wasn't sure whether I would have an NHL career, but I had played enough hockey to believe I deserved my chance.

Right after the Olympics, I signed with the Canadiens. I received a three-year deal for $110,000 per year and a $100,000 signing bonus. I bought a Ford Bronco with my signing bonus, because that's all I could afford.

The problem was my contract was in Canadian dollars, and the difference was about 40 cents on a dollar. Plus, Uncle Sam and the Canadian government each wanted their piece.

When I received my bonus check, the take-home pay was $28,000.

I went to general manager Serge Savard's office and pointed to the check.

"What's this?" I asked.

"It's called taxes," he said.

5

Lies, Half-truths, and Hockey

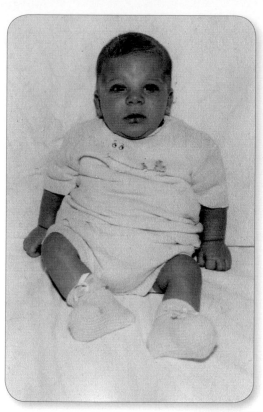

I was born in Chicago on January 25, 1962, and raised by my parents, Gus and Susan Chelios.

We lived in Evergreen Park, on the south side of the city, until I was in high school. That's when we moved to Southern California.

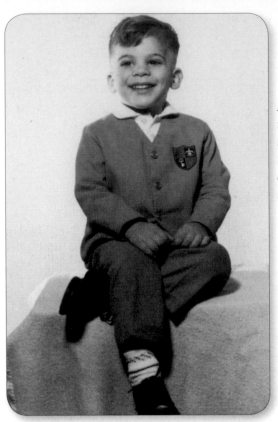

My dad owned a series of restaurants that both my mom and I worked at from time to time. He could be a demanding boss, to say the least.

Here are the Chelios kids: that's me holding my brother, Steve, along with our sisters (from left to right) Elena, Penny, and Gigi.

I played both hockey and baseball in Chicago, and was pretty good at both. I had a rivalry going with future MLB pitcher Donn Pall. I think we both chose the right sport.

My options for playing hockey in San Diego were limited. Here I am on that California team that wasn't good enough to even have a nickname.

I eventually caught the eye of some college programs, and signed my letter of intent to attend the University of Wisconsin.

Playing for head coach Badger Bob Johnson and his assistant Grant Standbrook was great for my career. I learned a lot about the game by listening to Standbrook and watching my teammate Bruce Driver.

After telling a little white lie, I found myself playing for the Moose Jaw Canucks up in Saskatchewan. And yes, our jersey was based on the traditional Blackhawks sweater. Funny how things turn out sometimes.

1984 United States
Canada Cup
Ice Hockey Team

HONORARY GENERAL MANAGER
TOMMY IVAN

GENERAL MANAGER
LOU NANNE
Met Center
7901 Cedar Avenue South
Bloomington, Minnesota 55420
(612) 853-9333

ASSISTANT GENERAL MANAGER
CRAIG PATRICK

EXECUTIVE DIRECTOR, AHAUS
HAL TRUMBLE
2997 Broadmoor Valley Road
Colorado Springs, Colorado 80906
(303) 576-4990

ADMINISTRATIVE ASSISTANT
ART BERGLUND

BUSINESS MANAGER
LARRY JOHNSON

PUBLIC RELATIONS DIRECTOR
DAVE FERRONI

PHYSICIAN
V. GEORGE NAGOBADS, MD

COACH
BOB JOHNSON
2997 Broadmoor Valley Road
Colorado Springs, Colorado 80906

ASSISTANT COACHES
TED SATOR
LOU VAIRO

TRAINER
SKIP THAYER

EQUIPMENT MANAGER
LARRY NESS

TEAM USA
CANADA CUP COMMITTEE
WALTER BUSH, JR., Chairman
BOB BUTERA
ROBERT FLEMING
GEORGE GUND
RALPH JASINSKI
ROBERT RIDDER
WILLIAM THAYER TUTT, Ex-Officio

MEMBER OF:
International Ice Hockey Federation
Amateur Hockey Association of the
   United States
United States Olympic Committee

July 11, 1984

Mr. Chris Chelios
1613 Capital Avenue
Madison, Wisconsin 53706

Dear Chris:

Please accept this letter as your official invitation to Team USA's 1984 Training Camp to be held this coming August in Colorado Springs and Bloomington, Minnesota.

You have been selected as one of thirty-two players who will be attending this Training Camp in preparation for the 1984 Canada Cup Tournament to be held September 1-September 18, 1984.

Each player attending the 1984 Training Camp will receive two-thousand dollars ($2,000). At the conclusion of Training Camp, each of those twenty-two players who are chosen to represent Team USA in the 1984 Canada Cup Tournament, will receive an additional two-thousand dollars ($2,000). Should Team USA be one of the two teams in the Canada Cup Finals, each player on the roster will receive an additional one-thousand dollars ($1,000). The players will each receive per diem in that amount which has been agreed to by the National Hockey League and the NHLPA for the upcoming 1984-85 season.

Training Camp will include six (6) exhibition games. Two games will be played at the Met Center in Bloomington, Minnesota, with the remaining four games being played in Montreal, Detroit, London and Edmonton.

Each player is requested to arrive in Colorado Springs on the evening of August 5th. Mr. Skip Trumble will be contacting you, if he has not already, regarding your travel to Colorado Springs. Training Camp will be held at the Air Force Academy, August 6th-August 12th. The players will be housed at the Antlers Hotel while in Colorado Springs. On the evening of August 12th, the team will travel to Minneapolis where they will be housed at the Bloomington Marriott until the conclusion of Training Camp. It should be noted that any players residing in the Twin Cities area, who may wish to reside at home, may do so.

1984 Canada Cup — September 1-20, 1984

I didn't really think about playing in the NHL until I was invited to play for Team USA in 1984, first in the Canada Cup (left) and then the Winter Olympics (below). That was a huge boost to my confidence.

1984 UNITED STATES HOCKEY TEAM

Front Row (L-R) Bob Mason, Mark Kumpel, Rich Costello, Phil Verchota, Lou Vairo (Coach), Walter Bush Jr. (Chairman), Larry Johnson (General Manager), John Harrington, Pat LaFontaine, Mark Fusco, Marc Behrend

Middle Row (L-R) Bob O'Connor (Ass't Coach), Dave Peterson (Ass't Coach), Doug Woog (Ass't Coach), Tim Taylor (Ass't Coach), Gary Sampson, Scott Fusco, Scott Bjugstad, Corey Millen, Tim Thomas, V. George Nagobads, M.D. (Physician), Sheldon Burns, M.D. (Physician), Dennis Helwig (Trainer), Buddy Kessel (Equipment Mgr.)

Back Row (L-R) Steve Griffith, David H. Jensen, Chris Chelios, Bob Brooke, Kurt Kleinendorst, Tom Hirsch, Al Iafrate, David A. Jensen, Ed Olczyk, Paul Guay, Gary Haight, Gene Barcikoski (Ass't Equipment Mgr.)

The Canada Cup in 1984 was the first time I'd been given the privilege of representing the United States. It was an honor I always cherished throughout my career. (Getty Images)

When you play for the Montreal Canadiens, there is nowhere to hide within the city limits.

Whatever you do, whomever you see, and wherever you go becomes public record. Every Montreal inhabitant, including coaches and reporters, seems to know everything about you or at least thinks they do. That's what I learned quickly after I started playing for the Canadiens in 1983–84.

When I signed with the team Bob Berry was the coach, but he was under so much pressure in the city when I arrived that I don't believe he uttered three words to me. I was dealing with my broken foot and couldn't play. About the time I was finally medically cleared, Berry was fired and replaced by Jacques Lemaire.

Lemaire was hard on me. He was a demanding guy. He benched me. A few times he embarrassed me. But I knew he was trying to make me a better player.

One time during a film session, Lemaire watched me make an ill-advised play, and then suddenly turned to me and asked, "Your girlfriend is in town, isn't she?"

The truth was he was right. Tracee, now my wife, came to see me once a month and that happened to be the weekend she was in town.

"Yes," I said, still not understanding the point he was about to make.

"I know, because every time she is in town your ankles are like this," he said, as he waved his hands back and forth.

I'm not sure whether he really knew or whether he was guessing, but unquestionably I was always more tired when Tracee was in town. I sent her home the next day.

My NHL career started out as well as I could have expected, other than the fact that I couldn't learn to one-time the puck. Lemaire repeatedly tried to teach me how execute the one-timer, and I simply couldn't master it. Sometimes I would connect and put a strong shot on net. But usually my timing was off by half a second.

I was competing against Bill Root, Dave Allison, and Ric Nattress for playing time as a right defenseman. It took me some time to adjust, but I was feeling comfortable by the time the play-offs came around.

The Canadiens barely qualified for the playoffs but we upset the Boston Bruins in the first round. Thankfully, Lemaire was giving me enough playing time to show what I could do. The more I played, the more comfortable I became. The same thing had happened in Moose Jaw and Wisconsin.

I scored my first NHL goal against Boston goalie Pete Peeters in that series. On the power play, I fired a shot from the point that zipped past him. Perry Turnbull supplied a screen in front.

Although no one was expecting much from us, it was still a disappointment when we were knocked out by the New York Islanders. Pat LaFontaine was on that Islanders squad. He had signed right after the Olympics. We won the first two games in that series and then lost four in a row.

IT WOULD NOT BE an exaggeration to say that it is impossible to have a private life and play for the Habs. You are recognized everywhere by everyone. I learned that very quickly.

Once while driving in downtown Montreal, I was idling at a red light when I witnessed a drunken man stagger and fall over as if he had dropped dead. Seeing his head slam on the cement, I jumped out of my car and went over to see if I could help.

When I reached him, he was unconscious, blood gushing from his wound. As I bent down to assist him, the inebriated man opened his eyes and said, "You're Chris Chelios!"

Even when you are living in strong American hockey markets such as Chicago and Detroit, you can still find places where you can escape your celebrity. You aren't recognized by everyone in an American city. But that isn't true in Canada, where fans can't get enough information about NHL teams and their players.

Playing in Montreal probably comes with the most pressure, partly because the team has a storied history of success. But it might also be because Montreal has both English-language and French-language media outlets, and they are constantly competing to generate the most information about the Habs.

Montreal's newspapers and radio and television stations reported on every move we made on and off the ice. In my seven seasons in Montreal, there were several stories that made it seem as if I was always in trouble with the team for carousing. It was certainly true that I liked to go out with the guys, and I was guilty of bad judgment on more than one occasion. But people should never believe everything they read in the newspapers or hear on the street.

It seemed as if there was an off-the-ice issue every season that was blown out of proportion. One season I was supposedly in a bar fight, when I was actually out with Tracee.

Another time there was a report of an after-hours car accident involving me that never happened.

Hockey is an obsession in Montreal, and every detail of your life is scrutinized by the press. It's impossible to run away or hide from the spotlight.

Once, general manager Serge Savard summoned me into his office and said that one of his friends had seen me in the famous Montreal strip club Chez Paree at 3:30 AM on the night before a game.

"I wasn't there," I insisted.

"But my friend saw you," Savard said.

"He could not have," I said, "because I was with Tracee."

"Why would my friend lie?" Savard asked.

"I don't know," I said. "But call my wife."

I'm not sure if he did; maybe he was just convinced by my offer.

Early in my career, Savard was always telling me that I needed to marry Tracee and settle down.

I didn't need him to tell me that, and we were married in 1988. Still, the rumors about my party life continued. I hated the lies worst of all because they had an impact on Tracee. It reached the point where I wanted to stay in my house out of fear that somebody would see me somewhere and suddenly I would be the lead story in the morning newspaper.

To be completely honest, while I probably didn't do half the things I was accused of, I do admit to having had a good time when I was young player in Montreal. In those days, few of us were choir boys. I roomed with fellow American Tom Kurvers early in my career, and it would be fair to say that we had an exceptionally good time together, except maybe when he played Bruce Springsteen's album *Born in the U.S.A.* so often that I almost wished I was Canadian.

Okay, maybe not, but I did throw that album in the trash to stop him from playing it. I like The Boss, but too much of any artist is never good.

Drinking with teammates was part of the hockey culture back then. Inside the mall located across from the Montreal Forum was a bar called the Brass Ring. It was the unofficial Canadiens bar. After practice, many of the players would head there to drink and unwind.

At dinner time, married players would go home, while the single guys would head to a restaurant together and then go out afterward. That's where you came together as a team. Most NHL coaches from that era would tell you that they liked it when their players drank together. As a general rule, it's better if players stick together than strike out on their own. Usually teammates will look after each other.

After the season, particularly if it didn't end well, Montreal players would leave town as quickly as possible. The fallout from a playoff loss can be harsh.

Once, after we were eliminated by the Bruins, I thought I was being smart by heading immediately for a Florida vacation. We left about 29 hours after the elimination, booking a pre-dawn flight to avoid crowds at the airport.

The taxi arrived at our downtown home and we climbed inside. As soon as we were seated, the driver turned around and showed Tracee and me his newspaper.

"It says here you are going to be traded," the cabbie said. "You packed pretty light, didn't you?"

The Canadiens were always more pleased with what I did on the ice than off the ice.

IN MY FIRST FEW seasons in Montreal, I did what most hockey players did in that era: I hung out with my teammates, especially on the road. When you boarded the plane the morning after a road game, everyone was hung over. That's just the way it was. Today, most players are too concerned about their conditioning levels to behave that way.

Playing cards was big with us in those days, but I am not much of a gambler. Early in my career, I was at a casino with Tracee and before I realized what was happening I had lost $5,000.

I was sick to my stomach about losing that money. All I could think was, *That could have paid for the fence we've been wanting to build around the house.*

Having grown up on Chicago's south side with a blue-collar mentality toward money, that day of blowing $5,000 was enough to kill any desire I may have had about being a frequent visitor to casinos. I've seen enough to know that gambling can send you tumbling down a deep, dark hole if you aren't careful.

When I've been in gambling situations since then, $500 is my limit. If I'm in Las Vegas, I will either win $500 or lose $500. That's how I view it.

When it comes to gambling, I simply don't have the balls to risk my money.

The only exception I've made to my $500 limit came years later at one of Michael Jordan's golf tournaments when I gave some money to Wayne Gretzky's wife, Janet, and told her that I wanted to "piggyback" off her at the blackjack table.

She used my money, along with hers, and won me $14,000.

Despite my disinterest in playing for high stakes, I did enjoy going to the casinos and hanging out with the guys as they gambled. And no one was more fun to go to the casino with than the late Bob Probert.

One night Probie was winning at the blackjack table before baseball Hall of Famer Reggie Jackson pulled up a chair and sat down.

Obviously a new player changes how the cards are dealt out, and suddenly the dealer started winning most of the hands. With Mr. October sitting there, Probie's luck went south.

Probie was grumpy about that turn of events, to say the least, and he became more unhappy when Jackson had the courage to criticize one of Probert's decisions.

"You know what?" Probie said to Jackson. "Go fuck yourself. I was doing fine until you sat down."

Jackson looked at him for a second and then walked away from the table. It was a winning moment for Probert. Nobody forced Probert to back off, not even a Hall of Famer at a blackjack table.

In Montreal, John Kordic, Mike Keane, Shayne Corson, Claude Lemieux, and I had a regular game. Once, in Philadelphia, we thought that we had caught Lemieux cheating.

We were walking into the rink, and I was talking about it with Lemieux.

"That was bullshit," I said.

He spit at me, then grabbed me and ripped my shirt in the process. Corson jumped in. The fighting escalated. We were going at it in the dressing room when Lemaire walked in. As soon as he discovered that the fight was over a card game, he banned card playing.

Embarrassed by what happened, I vowed I never would play cards with teammates again. Lemieux and I worked out our differences, and we were able to get along.

Another time, Lemaire and assistant coach Jacques Laperriere did a curfew check during a road trip to Vancouver, calling all of our rooms.

Eight of us didn't answer. Guy Carbonneau and Chris "Knuckles" Nilan were among them. I was rooming with young defenseman Petr Svoboda, and we had also been out on the town.

Word filtered around that we would all be benched in the next game, and Petr was nervous. He said his girlfriend was going to be mad at him once she found out he had been benched for violating curfew. She was going to want to know where he was.

We purposely avoided the coaches that morning, and then Petr and I convinced the people at the front desk to clandestinely move us to a different room.

With our alibi ironed out, we marched off to see Laperriere and ask him what was up. He said he had personally dialed our room and there was no answer.

We vehemently insisted that we had been in our room in time for bed check. Finally, I asked him which room he had called, and he told me.

"That's the problem," I said. "That's not our room number."

We showed him our room keys and he accepted our explanation. We played the next game. Nilan wasn't too happy with us.

When I wasn't out having a good time with them, I was learning a lot from my teammates, especially the veterans. When you sit in the same dressing room with Larry Robinson and Bob Gainey, it's like receiving a master's degree in hockey. I was in an institution of higher learning when it came to my sport.

I learned how to be a leader by watching those guys every day. I watched how they played and also how they treated people. I admired how calm Gainey was, no matter what was going on with our team. Gainey lived two blocks from me in Montreal, and I always listened to everything he had to say.

Once, we were beating the New York Islanders 6–2 at Nassau Coliseum and I was pushing up into the play, still trying to score goals. I was playing angry and stupid hockey because Islanders star defenseman Denis Potvin had gone after my knees.

After I made a dash up ice, Gainey skated over to me and said simply, "You know, our team doesn't need that seventh goal."

I've never forgotten those words or that lesson. A coach could have lectured me for an hour and not had the same impact that Gainey had with a single, succinct sentence.

Other veterans such as Steve Shutt, Mario Tremblay, and Rick Green also helped me along the way. The Canadiens dressing room was an exceptional learning center.

Chris Nilan was one of my best friends in Montreal. He took me under his wing and looked after me. We lived in the same building right across from the Forum. Whether I wanted to go or not, Nilan took me with him everywhere. He would tell me we were going somewhere and I would be too afraid to say no. As everyone now knows, he was a bad drinker, and his issues spilled over on me sometimes.

I wasn't the only person scared of him. He made the 1987 U.S. team in the Canada Cup because no one wanted to tell him he was cut.

That's a true story. Badger Bob Johnson was the coach, and he thought about keeping young Jimmy Carson over Nilan. But Johnson said he wasn't going to be the one to tell Nilan, and no one else wanted to do it either. So Johnson kept him. The funny ending to the story is that Chris scored a pair of goals in the tournament.

The best story about Nilan in that tournament involved his confrontation with Rick Vaive in a greasy diner near the Montreal Forum.

The Americans had a game against Canada and Chris hit someone. So Vaive came over and two-handed Nilan over the head. Nilan didn't have the opportunity during the game to get his revenge.

The next morning, Nilan, Neal Broten, and I entered the diner to have breakfast and discovered half of the Canadian team was there.

Both Broten and I knew immediately this was trouble.

Sure enough, Nilan walked directly up to Vaive and said, "What the hell were you doing, hitting me over the head?"

"Fuck you, cement head," Vaive said. It was not the smartest choice of words he ever made.

Nilan took his open hand and drilled him in the face. I immediately thought that we were going to get killed stepping in to help Nilan.

But stunningly, not one member of the Canadian team rose up to challenge him.

We just walked out of the place and headed to the Forum. Within 15 minutes, everyone in Montreal knew the story. Hockey news travels at the speed of light in Montreal. Luckily, nothing ever came of it.

Nilan was an important member of our team when I first arrived, but his drinking habits cost him. He would be the first to tell you that. He lost his place on the top line and he became an angry man. The Canadiens traded him in 1987–88.

Another lesson I learned in Montreal is that while a person can change, his reputation may not. After I married Tracee and we had our first child, Dean, in 1989, I realized how much I had changed when I was over at Svoboda's house once and we were both feeding our kids instead of going out on the town.

Looking to give Tracee a break from parenting duties, I started bringing Dean to the Habs dressing room when he was just a few months old. That was the season I missed half of the year because of knee surgery and was coming to the Forum to do rehab work every day. I left a fold-up playpen in my Forum locker. I would put Dean in the playpen and lift weights, or pedal the stationary bike with Dean on my lap.

Sports Illustrated published a story about the changes in my life titled "Daddy Dearest: Award-winning Chris Chelios of Montreal is a nasty cuss on the ice, but playing the role of parent has helped him develop a softer side."

My opponents would probably disagree.

AS CHALLENGING AS IT was to be a Montreal Canadien 24 hours a day, the advantages I had playing there could not be ignored. When my NHL career was only 127 games old, I won my first Stanley Cup.

The 1985–86 Canadiens were certainly a surprise winner. We were the seventh-place team that season, and in the Stanley Cup Final we knocked off the sixth-place Calgary Flames.

For us to reach the championship series, the right teams fell at the right time, and young players stepped up at the right time. The big story that season was that we were playing with eight rookies in the lineup. Robinson got sick of hearing about it.

"I've been hearing about our rookies all series," he told the media. "I was a rookie, too, once. That isn't an excuse to make a mistake. When I came here, I wasn't looking for Frank Mahovlich or Serge Savard or Guy Lapointe to play for me. I worked my butt off to prove to them that I belonged up here, that I could do the job myself. It's the same way with these guys. We're all just hockey players. We're all in this together."

If you asked me to provide two reasons why we won that season, I would say goalie Patrick Roy and forward Claude Lemieux.

When we think of Roy, we think of a vocal, charismatic leader. But he was just a humble kid when he was piling up wins for us in 1986.

Larry Robinson told the media that Roy's goaltending was the best he had ever seen, and that was coming from a guy who had played six seasons with Ken Dryden.

Lemieux had only played 19 games when the playoffs started, and proceeded to score 10 goals in 20 playoff games.

I had eight goals and 26 assists for 34 points in 41 games before my injury, and then I came back in the playoffs and contributed as best I could.

The height of my popularity in Montreal probably came when I won my first Norris Trophy in 1988–89. I was also fifth in the Hart Trophy race that season. We reached the Stanley Cup Final, where we lost to the Flames.

That following season my teammates voted me captain to replace the retired Bob Gainey. Guy Carbonneau was made the co-captain, because it was felt we needed to have a French-speaking leader to deal with the media. It was the right decision by Savard and coach Pat Burns. When I was a young player, a few of us had taken French lessons out of respect for the culture of the city. But we didn't stick with it long enough to acquire any ability to speak or understand it.

In hindsight, I wasn't ready to be a captain at that time. The responsibility overwhelmed me and it affected my performance. Serving as captain for a storied franchise like the Canadiens required a maturity and poise that I didn't yet have.

I wasn't even sure how the fans in Montreal felt about my being captain because I couldn't read French. My friend and famed *Montreal Gazette* columnist Red Fisher would inform me if there was an urgent matter that needed to be addressed, but it was frustrating to be a one-language captain for a bilingual NHL team.

Most people know that the most famous and most devastating hit I ever delivered was against Philadelphia Flyers forward Brian Propp during the 1989 Stanley Cup playoffs.

What people may not know is that I went after him in retaliation for a two-handed slash that broke two of my fingers during the regular season.

Propp was a chippy player, not unlike a lot of other guys in that era. I never said a word to the media when he broke my fingers. I just figured I would get him back at the appropriate time.

In Game 1 of the Wales Conference Final, I threw an elbow into his head and it snapped back into one of the metal stanchions that hold the Plexiglas in place. He was unconscious as he went down, and somewhere in the process of being hit and landing on the ice he ended up with a gash on the back of his head.

No penalty was assessed on the play, and NHL vice president Brian O'Neill deemed that no suspension was warranted. His ruling was that I hadn't meant to hurt Propp.

That was partly true—I had not intended to hurt Propp that badly. But there was no question that I had targeted him with intent to cause him some pain.

Sports Illustrated wrote that I hit Propp "with a flying elbow that would have done Jack Tatum proud."

At the end of that series, Flyers goalie Ron Hextall came after me and ended up being suspended 12 games for the attack. That seemed like a lot of games to me, given that he didn't inflict any real damage. I saw him coming, and the only reason I couldn't fully protect myself was because Philadelphia defenseman Kjell Samuelsson had kicked my skates out from under me just before Hextall arrived. As soon as Hextall swung at me, I grabbed him and put him into a headlock.

I said that the NHL was only coming down hard on Hextall because he was a goalie. League officials clearly didn't want it to become commonplace for goalies to believe they needed to stick up for their teammates.

Truthfully, I admired Hextall for standing up for Propp. If I had been a goalie and something like that had happened to one of my teammates, I probably would have done exactly what Hextall did. Over the years, I've run into Hextall and he has always been courteous toward me about the situation. He told me once he appreciated that I never made a big deal about it.

A few years after the Propp incident, I ran into him at a bar in Madison, Wisconsin. He was dating Scott Mellanby's sister at the time, and Propp and I ended up talking and hanging out all night. We had plenty of laughs. Propp was also with me the next day on a boat. Someone snapped a photograph that included Propp and me clearly having a good time.

I wish I'd had a copy of that photo a couple years later when Propp had some negative things to say about me. I could have shown it around and asked, "Does it look like he has no use for me?"

When I played in Montreal, my archenemy was actually Dale Hunter, not Propp. On the ice, I hated him, especially when he played for the Quebec Nordiques. He was a great player who scored an impressive number of important goals. But he hurt me a couple of times, hit me from behind more than once, and once blew my knee out.

I tried to hit him but I never really hurt him, not like he got me. Once, I was coming across the blue line and was watching my shot after I had really cranked one.

Then I woke up in the Montreal dressing room.

My first words were, "Let me guess—Dale Hunter?"

Another time, there were 30 seconds left in the game and Hunter was chasing me around the ice waving his stick at me. He was swinging like he was trying to drive a fastball over the center-field fence. Fortunately, I never let him catch me. I have that one on tape.

However, Hunter definitely had the upper hand in our long feud. We met once in a bar and looked at each other, but didn't say much.

NEVER DURING MY SEVEN seasons in Montreal did I ever ask to be traded. As difficult as it was for me to play there, I enjoyed the atmosphere. I liked my teammates. I liked the city. I loved playing for an organization that expected to be a contender every season.

However, it was no secret that someday, somehow, I wanted to play for the Chicago Blackhawks.

Early in the 1988–89 season, the *Chicago Tribune* published a story quoting me as saying I "wouldn't be crying" if the Canadiens dealt me to the Blackhawks.

"I love Montreal and the Canadiens have treated me first-class, but Chicago is where my heart is," I told *Tribune* writer Mike Kiley.

I can imagine how that story played with Montreal fans.

Chicago general manager Bob Pulford admitted the interest was mutual.

"We'd love to have Chelios," Pulford told the *Tribune* on November 18, 1988. "But it would be difficult to make a trade for a good player like that. I've explored the availability in the past and I'd be willing to seriously look at him again if he was ever available."

It was true that it would have been challenging for the Blackhawks to acquire me. In 1987–88, I had scored 20 goals and finished with 61 points and 172 penalty minutes. I was sixth in the Norris Trophy race. I was 26 and entering the prime of my career. It wasn't totally unthinkable that the Canadiens would trade me if they believed my nightlife escapades were wilder than they really were. But to make a trade of that magnitude, the Canadians would have to acquire a player that would appease the fan base.

As it happened, the Blackhawks had such a player. It was center Denis Savard, a dynamic French Canadian scoring machine who had produced 44 goals and generated 131 points in 1987–88.

He also had the "wow" factor in his game. He had a spin-o-rama move and magic in his hands. He was just a year older than me, meaning he also was in the prime of his career.

It seemed like both teams could sell the trade to their fans as one team wanting to add a scorer and the other team needing to add a defenseman. Mike Keenan became the coach in Chicago in 1988, and my playing style fit his coaching style more than Savard's did.

The problem was that Chicago owner Bill Wirtz loved Savard. It seemed like the two sides were at an impasse and that I'd be a Canadien for the foreseeable future.

Jailhouse
Rocked

On the day that Chicago coach and general manager Mike Keenan worked diligently to put me in a Blackhawks jersey, police officers in Madison, Wisconsin, were working just as hard to put me behind bars.

It's true—I was in jail, along with Gary Suter, for fighting police officers early in the morning on June 29, 1990, the day Keenan and Montreal general manager Serge Savard negotiated the trade that sent me from Montreal to Chicago for popular center Denis Savard.

It had been a crazy 48-hour period. I wonder how many NHL players have been incarcerated and traded in the same 24-hour news cycle. Neither event had anything to do with the other.

And to think, that day started with Sutes and me trying to do everything by the book.

I first met Suter back at the University of Wisconsin. He was on a recruiting trip and was out on the town drinking with other recruits and Badger players. We were all walking down Langdon Street, near the fraternities, and no one seemed to notice that Sutes was trailing 15 feet behind the pack.

Suddenly, there was a loud crash and we turned to see that Suter had thrown a chair through a storefront window for no

apparent reason. We certainly didn't stick around long to speculate—we all took off before the police arrived.

That's my first memory of Suter. At that point, I knew nothing
about him except that his brother Bob had played on the 1980
Olympic team. But I quickly learned that Gary was a very quiet,
unassuming player who became a wildly different human being
when he drank.

When he was drinking, he would call himself Gerald; that
was his alter ego. Gary didn't drink and do all of that damage.
It was Gerald. We all had fun with both Gary and Gerald Suter.

He did some crazy stuff, and usually I was with him. Gerald
was an instigator. He would start drinking and things in hotel
rooms would end up broken. We could be driving down the
street and Suter would grab your watch and throw it out the
window.

People always talk about how I was a well-conditioned athlete,
but Suter was in much better shape than I was. I know that is true
because we trained together in the summer, running the steps at
Randall Stadium. Suter had it all figured out: if he sprinted up
the stairs in 12 seconds and walked back down in 45 seconds,
it was like a shift in hockey. It was a 3:1 or 4:1 ratio. He would
repeat that process over and over and over.

When he took the VO2 test they gave us in training camp, he
always scored off the charts.

He was always nervous before big games but he played hard
and his numbers were always exceptional.

Suter also had an on-off switch when it came to his temper,
whether he was on the ice or off of it. You definitely wanted to get
out of the way if Suter reached his boiling point because he could
scald you. He was meaner and scarier than he looked.

I remember Dale Hunter didn't know anything about Suter and decided to pick on him. The Suter switch went to the 'on' position and he knocked out a bunch of Hunter's teeth with a single punch. It didn't look like much if you saw it live, but Hunter was totally surprised to be standing there with a big gap where his teeth had been.

Jocelyn Lemieux also got Suterized one night. He took a run at Gary but Gary simply cross-checked him in the face. Lemieux also ended up with fewer teeth as a penalty for wronging Suter.

When we played together at the 1987 Canada Cup, Suter was speared by Andrei Lomakin of the Soviet Union. The switch went on, and Suter tomahawked Lomakin in the face with his stick. The force of the blow was strong enough that Suter's stick snapped in half. I don't believe Suter knew what he was doing once he became incensed by Lomakin's spear.

Lomakin needed 20 stitches to close the wound and Suter received a six-game suspension from the International Ice Hockey Federation and four more games from the NHL.

Four years later, at the Canada Cup, he knocked Wayne Gretzky out of the tournament with a check from behind. I don't believe he intended to hurt Gretzky, but he became Public Enemy No. 1 in Canada. He even received death threats.

The first person we saw the next day when we walked into the rink was Gretzky, who had his arm in a sling, and Suter walked right up to him and apologized.

The whole thing bothered Suter immensely, because he was the kind of player who didn't like being the center of attention. He was the kind of guy who liked to sit alone at the end of the bar making cynical comments about what was happening elsewhere.

I always said he would much rather be alone, sitting in a deer blind, than stand in the spotlight. He didn't play hockey to be the guy everyone talked about. He wanted to do his job and be left alone.

ON THE DAY OF the trade, Suter and I were in Madison for a golf tournament, but rain delayed the event. As was often the case when given time to kill, we drank while we waited for the weather to improve. By the end of the day, Sutes and I were shitfaced. Knowing we shouldn't drive, we took cabs back downtown.

The cab pulled up to Lundeen's Bar on Fairchild, and I jumped out of the cab and told the cabbie to wait because I had to pee. When I have to pee, I have to go right then. That's just the way I've always been.

I ducked into the alley and started to piss on the side of a building. I noticed there was another guy in the alley doing exactly the same thing.

"What's up," I said.

He nodded, I finished my business, and then I headed back to the cab to pay my fare. Just as I handed over the cash, the guy from the alley tapped me on the shoulder and said he needed to see some identification.

"Why?" I asked, not sure what he was talking about.

"I need to see some identification because you were urinating in public," he said.

Then he pulled out his badge to identify himself as a police officer.

I was drunk, but seeing the badge sobered me up in a hurry.

"What are you talking about?" I said. "You were pissing right next to me."

"I'm plain clothes, working undercover," he said.

My inebriated mind struggled to accept the notion that I'd been caught in a sting operation set up to catch men who have to pee. It seems funny now, but it wasn't then.

"You are fucking going to jail," he said.

"Fuck you," I said. "No, I am not."

He went to grab me but I pulled away from him. Thankfully, even in my drunken state I knew enough not to hit him. In addition to the obvious legal ramifications, I was only a month out from having hernia surgery, and I didn't want to tear open my stomach. Suddenly, another officer jumped me and I had two cops wrestling me on the sidewalk.

Apparently, someone had yelled into the bar that two guys had jumped me, so Suter came flying out the door and decked one of the cops. He had no idea who he was hitting.

"Sutes, stop!" I yelled. "They are cops."

"Shit," he said.

One of the cops tried to show Suter his badge, but I immediately grabbed it and started running down the street with it.

Half a block away, I looked back and saw Suter getting killed. Now, there were three cop cars on the scene. "Fuck," I said, and turned around to head back to the scene of the crime. I jumped right into the middle of the pile.

As you can imagine, Suter and I got our asses kicked. Then, we got arrested.

On the way to the station, the cop with the missing badge told me he wanted it back. I told him that I threw it away as I was running down the street. The truth was that it was stuffed down my pants.

"You are going to be strip searched, so you may as well give it up," he said.

As it turned out, the cop had the names of his snitches written on the back of his badge, which was why he was quite concerned about getting it back.

My theft of the badge turned out to be a saving grace: Suter was able to say that he never saw a badge and therefore didn't know the guys who had their hands on me were cops. He believed he was helping a friend who was being mugged.

I was able to leave jail quickly because I was not charged with assaulting an officer. I was able to use my credit card to pay my bail. Suter had to spend the night in jail.

After going home for a good night's sleep, I was awakened by a call from Serge Savard.

"I guess you heard," I said.

"Heard what?" he asked.

"I was arrested yesterday," I said.

"That's okay," he said, "because I traded you last night."

"Where?" I asked.

"Chicago," he said.

That's when I realized that I had mixed emotions about the deal. I had spent seven fun seasons in Montreal, and I was sad about leaving the Canadiens. I told Serge that.

"Well," he said. "I could have really fucked you and traded you to Winnipeg for Dale Hawerchuk."

"In that case, thanks!" I said, as we both laughed.

Serge Savard didn't give me a straight answer on why he moved me. He would only say that people were "on his back" to make a move.

For many years, I wondered whether I had been dealt because of a false rumor that had spread around the city about my having an affair with the wife of Canadiens president Ronald Corey.

That rumor had started because Mrs. Corey was seen coming to my house on numerous occasions. The reality was we lived around the corner from the Coreys, and she came to our house to check on my wife. We were alone in Montreal, and Mrs. Corey was simply trying to make sure Tracee was doing okay.

Then I was seen talking to her once on the street, and the next day it was in the newspaper. Some hockey player in Quebec even wrote a song saying I was screwing Corey's wife.

Montreal is a tremendous city and great hockey town, but it can be a difficult place to live. It felt as if the French Canadian media was out to get me. Red Fisher was the only member of the media who was trying to protect me. It seemed offensive to a lot of people in the media that I was an American-born captain of their beloved Habs.

The reporters treated French Canadian players far differently than they treated the English-speaking players. Guy Carbonneau would get into trouble away from the rink, and it wasn't nearly the story that it was when I had a couple of issues. It felt as if the media wanted to bury me.

Remember, I was playing in Montreal at a time when the separatist movement was thriving. The idea of Quebec seceding from Canada had energy and support. We had a good team, and yet there were members of the media who felt the franchise needed to do more to embrace the French Canadian tradition in its signings and hiring practices.

Seven Americans were on the 1985–86 Stanley Cup championship team. Yet David Maley, Steve Rooney, and Tom Kurvers were gone soon after and the rest followed them out the door.

When I was inducted into the Hockey Hall of Fame in 2013, I was surprised to see Serge Savard there. I saw him sitting in the lobby with Montreal-based sportswriter Michael Farber.

I asked Serge whether I could have a minute with him, and he obliged.

"Just tell me the truth," I said. "Did you trade me because of that rumor?"

"No," he said. "I knew it wasn't true."

He told me the truth about what happened but he asked me not to reveal it. I will honor his wishes here. However, I can say that what he said finally gave me peace of mind 23 years after the deal was completed.

ALTHOUGH I LIKED PLAYING for the Canadiens, it was time for me to leave. I had just married Tracee and we had our first child, Dean, on the way.

Regardless of why I was traded, it was a big deal in the hockey world.

This was an old-school swap that had fans in both countries buzzing. I had won the Norris Trophy two seasons earlier and Denis Savard was a dazzling center who had registered 80 points in 60 games. I was 28 and he was 29.

I hate when team politics interfere with hockey decisions, but this deal had a lot of issues bubbling beneath the surface. It wasn't just a matter of Keenan trading away an offensive player to acquire a defensive player. Keenan and Savard didn't get along, and Keenan had wanted to trade Savard during the 1989–90 NHL season. However, Chicago owner Bill Wirtz vetoed the idea. According to the *Chicago Tribune*, Wirtz viewed Savard as a player who got fans buying tickets whether the team was winning or losing.

Savard was a gifted player with a crowd-pleasing style. He could bring you out of your seat with some of his moves and made defensemen look foolish on a regular basis. But Keenan wasn't interested in guys who were magicians with the puck or had eyes in the backs of their heads. He wanted warriors. He wanted to run opponents into the boards and then right out of the building.

Not long before he traded for me, then–Edmonton Oilers captain Mark Messier had come into Chicago Stadium and turned around a playoff series against the Blackhawks through physical intimidation.

The Blackhawks had a 2–1 lead in the best-of-seven Western Conference Final. If the Blackhawks won Game 4, they'd probably win the series.

But Messier had other ideas. He let his intentions be known on his first shift when he broke his stick across Steve Larmer's arm.

Keenan said after the game that Messier could have been called for "15 stick infractions." The *Tribune* quoted Blackhawks winger Steve Thomas as saying Messier was "wielding his stick like a mad man."

Messier also scored a pair of goals in that game to lead the Oilers to a 4–2 win that tied the series 2–2. When you look back at that postseason, Messier's ruthless performance against the Blackhawks may have been the turning point.

So it certainly seemed as if Keenan was looking to add players who would make sure something like that would never happen again. And clearly, I wasn't uncomfortable playing in a game where stick work was in play.

In my four previous seasons with the Canadiens, I had averaged better than 150 penalty minutes per season. I wasn't accumulating all of those minutes for hooking and holding. I played with an edge, just like Messier did.

Even though I was back in Chicago, I still couldn't escape the passion of the Canadiens fans. After the trade, I ran into two Montreal fans at the Lodge Bar on Division Street. These guys were riding me, accusing me of hating French-speaking people.

I tried to keep the banter friendly, pointing out that it was the Canadiens who had decided to trade me. It was not my decision to leave.

The discussion continued to escalate until one of the fans asked me to step outside.

"I'm not fighting you," I said. "You would sue me. I have too much to lose."

Then I had an idea. I told the guy to fetch a pen and a piece of paper and write CHRIS CHELIOS IS IN NO WAY RESPONSIBLE FOR THIS FIGHT. IT WAS MY IDEA TO FIGHT CHELIOS.

The Montreal fan, who was about my age, agreed and carefully crafted his letter and signed it. I read it and then asked to see his driver's license so I knew he was who he said he was.

As he reached for his identification, I sucker-punched him square in his jaw. He was knocked out cold.

"That was a cheap shot," his friend said.

"Yep," I said. "And I have his signed letter saying he asked for it."

The bartender and the doorman were howling with laughter. Finally, they threw the two guys out of the bar. My victim eventually regained his senses and started banging on the window. I just held up his letter and laughed at him. After a while someone called the police. We knew all of the cops around there, and when they showed up they asked if we wanted the two guys arrested.

"No," I said. "Just take them five blocks away and drop them off."

NOT LONG BEFORE I was traded, I had signed a three-year contract extension that paid me about $1.1 million per season, with some of the money deferred. For the season I had just played in Montreal, for example, I had a base salary of around $550,000 and would receive two more payments of roughly $275,000 in the seventh and eighth year after the contract was signed.

Adding deferred money to contracts started to gain popularity in the NHL once player salaries really started to climb. In theory, owners can end up paying less that way, because they could set aside less money than they actually owe in an annuity, or some other form of investment, and use part of the interest they earn to pay off their future obligation.

That was fine with me, because knowing I was going to have that money coming in down the line was appealing. I was 28 when I signed that deal, and I was going to be getting that money when I was 35 and 36. At that point, I certainly didn't know I would be playing in the NHL well past that time. In that era, 35 was ancient for a player.

Also, I had watched my dad experience financial troubles when I was a kid. Those memories stuck with me, and I certainly didn't want to put my wife and family through a bunch of personal and financial upheaval if I could avoid it. I wanted a secure future.

This was before the NHLPA had full salary disclosure, and I remember Paul Coffey came by the Montreal Forum to ask me what I was making. Boston's Ray Bourque did the same. Of course, I told them the truth because I thought it was the right thing to do. As it turned it out, we were all making about the same.

But unlike most owners, Bill Wirtz of the Blackhawks didn't believe in putting deferred money into contracts. It didn't seem like it would be a problem until we sat down to calculate the final numbers. I don't recall the dollar figures down to the penny, but I remember that the Blackhawks determined that the present-day value of my contract was just over $700,000 per season.

What they were saying, in essence, was that the Canadiens had paid me $550,000 and put roughly $150,000 into an annuity that they expected would grow into the $550,000 they owed me down the line. Since the Blackhawks didn't defer money, they wanted to just give me $700,000 and allow me to invest it myself.

Another sticking point was that I had already played one season under my arrangement with Montreal. Wirtz was trying to say that those deferred payments were now the Blackhawks' responsibility, but again, since they didn't do deferred payments, they wanted to figure out the present-day value of the two $275,000 payments I was owed and add it to my contract moving forward.

That didn't sit well with me. My position was that Montreal owed me that deferred money for the season that was already played. It was locked in and shouldn't have any bearing on my revised contract with the Blackhawks. I wanted those deferred payments when I was in my thirties, not to take the cash equivalent right then and there.

Essentially, the argument came down to the Blackhawks saying that even though the contract I signed called for me to be paid $1.1 million per year counting the deferred payments, what the Canadiens were actually paying out of pocket, prior to accruing interest, was closer to $700,000, and so that's what they were willing to pay per year.

That led to an 11-hour, smoke-filled negotiation in Mr. Wirtz's office. The meeting included me, Mr. Wirtz, Bob Pulford, Mike Keenan, and Don Meehan, who was my agent at the time.

Three times during the meeting I got up to walk out and said I would live with the existing terms of my contract, which included the deferred money.

"Wait a minute, wait a minute," Mr. Wirtz would mumble.

Then he, Pulford, and Keenan would leave the room to discuss their strategy.

For all I know, those guys all walked out the door and then went to the bathroom. I think they just wanted to leave Meehan and me in the room to think about the situation. I think they were trying to make me anxious. I wasn't.

After about 30 minutes, they would come back in the room and we would continue talking.

All of those guys were smoking back then, and the smoke was annoying me more than anything they were saying. On top of everything else, I had no idea how long this negotiation was going to last and I had my son Dean with me. He wasn't even two years old yet, and I had left him with one of the secretaries in the office at 9:00 AM.

Finally, they agreed to the $1.1 million base pay, but I had to agree to add a year onto my contract. When we were finished, Mr. Wirtz stood up and said, "Let's go downstairs and have a drink."

"Chris can't because we have a game tomorrow," Keenan said.

We were scheduled to play the Vancouver Canucks, and Keenan wanted me to be sharp. At the time, I was in the midst of a lengthy goal-scoring slump. I don't think the uncertainty over my contract was a distraction. I think it was just one of those things.

"Screw that," Mr. Wirtz said. "We are going to have a drink."

"I can't drink," I said. "I have to drive home with my kid."

"We will call a car to take you home and you can pick up your car tomorrow," Mr. Wirtz said.

Mr. Wirtz was not a guy who liked taking no for an answer.

"What are you drinking?" Mr. Wirtz asked.

"Scotch," I said for no apparent reason. I had never drunk Scotch in my life.

Everyone poured down a drink, and then two and then three. We all got happy quickly. The more we drank the better a story-teller Mr. Wirtz became. Soon it was midnight, and Mr. Wirtz acted like we were just getting started. Finally, I convinced him that I had to get my son home, not to mention that I had to play an NHL game in 19 hours.

Of course, I played a great game against Vancouver and scored a goal to break my slump. Apparently a nightcap with the boss was all I needed. Mr. Wirtz loved me after that.

The issue about Montreal owing me money, however, continued to bug me. Finally I called Serge Savard's secretary, Donna Stewart, in Montreal and she confirmed that the team had no record of owing that money to me.

Adding that extra year to my contract at Chicago's behest definitely cost me some money because I won my second Norris Trophy in 1992–93. I should have been negotiating a new contract on the heels of that trophy. Instead, I played the next season for $1.1 million.

By then, the Blackhawks were talking to me about a new contract. It was no secret. NHLPA executive director Bob Goodenow heard about it and showed up at my home unannounced. He asked me to play out my contract and then become a free agent, believing that I could command more money on the open market and set a new standard for the next wave of free agents. He didn't like Mr. Wirtz and thought Chicago should be paying its players more. Goodenow was all worked up, swearing about Mr. Wirtz and swearing at me.

"Look, Bob, you have other guys fighting the fight," I said. "But my situation is different. I'm in my hometown. I've already been traded once and I don't want to move again."

At first, he wouldn't take no for an answer. He kept pounding away at me, saying I needed to do it for the good of the other players.

"If I wasn't in Chicago, I would do it in a heartbeat," I said. "But this is where I want to be. My parents are here."

I know Goodenow was just doing his job. He was not happy with me, but when I look back at that situation, I made the right decision for me and my family.

Later, news got back to me that Goodenow was ripping my decision to all of the other players, claiming that I was a "walking salary cap." He said the same thing about Raymond Bourque, who also accepted less money because he liked playing in Boston.

My position was that Bourque and I were established veteran players who had earned the right to stay where we were if that was what we wanted. At that point in my life, I didn't feel like I needed more money as much I needed the stability of living in Chicago.

Goodenow had a new army of young, militant players (with no wives or kids) who were ready to fight the fight.

Bourque took the Bruins to arbitration in the summer of 1993, and I was waiting for that verdict before I signed my new deal with the Blackhawks.

The Bruins were only offering $1.85 million per season and Bourque was asking for a salary in the range of $4 million to $4.5 million per season. Bruins general manager Harry Sinden said at the time that he might trade Bourque if the arbitrator's award was too high.

Most of the players in the NHL were stunned on the day the 1993–94 season opened, when arbitrator Richard Bloch made an award of $2.25 million per season on a two-year contract for Bourque. It was a clear win for the Bruins. The NHL's arbitration process was not like the process in Major League Baseball, where the arbitrator had to pick one offer or the other. Bloch was allowed to pick a third number, one he believed was a compromise—and one that was much closer to the Bruins' number.

We heard that the arbitrator didn't believe Bourque was worth what he was asking for because he wasn't physically aggressive enough. Are you kidding me?

On the day after the Bourque ruling was delivered, Pulford was waiting for me in the dressing room.

"You are going to have to sign for what we are offering now," he said in his gravelly voice.

He was right. If Bourque's request for $4 million was shot down, anything I suggested in that range would be too. I ended up signing a three-year contract that paid me $2.65 million, $2.75 million, and $2.8 million.

While Goodenow wasn't able to convince me to undertake the commando mission on behalf of my fellow players, there were many who did, such as Keith Tkachuk and Eric Lindros. We all benefited from the fact that they had the balls to sit out. But like I said, I have no regrets about my decision.

I was just happy to be home.

7

Mayhem on Madison

The Chicago Blackhawks played tough, physical hockey under coach Mike Keenan in the early 1990s.

We were even rougher and wilder in the dressing room and during practice.

When I played for the Blackhawks, practices occasionally would have to be suspended because they devolved into brawls between teammates.

Defenseman Dave Manson, still in his skates, once chased Keenan out of the dressing room because he had finally gotten fed up with Keenan's constant criticism. Keenan belittled him once too often, and Manson flew off his dressing room seat and bolted toward Keenan with rage in his eyes. Keenan fled to the safety in his office. I have no idea what would have happened had Manson caught him.

Another time at practice, I remember defenseman Bryan Marchment and tough guy Stu Grimson trading punches, and then Jeremy Roenick jumped in to help Marchment. Darryl Sutter didn't appreciate Roenick butting in, and he started to throw punches at Roenick. The situation deteriorated from there. Others joined in and chaos followed.

On another occasion, Manson buzzed goalie Eddie Belfour during a practice with a high shot near his mask. The next time

Manson came down the ice on a drill he found Belfour waiting for him with his goalie stick raised like a tomahawk.

Those two fought ferociously at center ice like they were gladiators in the Colosseum.

When Keenan was coach, the Chicago Stadium truly was a Madhouse on Madison. Most of the players understood that Keenan liked his players to have their emotions just below the boiling point. He wanted the tension level high because he felt it kept us on edge.

The problem is when guys are always running in the red, tempers can get short, even among teammates.

In Montreal, the Canadiens were always trying to persuade me to reduce the number of undisciplined penalties I took. In Chicago, Keenan liked me to push the rules as far as I could.

Many times while playing for the Blackhawks, I was kicked out of games in the third period because I was trying to get even with someone or wanted to show the fans that I cared.

That's the way it was in the 1990s, and that's certainly the way Keenan liked us to play. Back then, the skilled players were not as big and tough as they are today. It was possible to rattle some of the top players if you bullied them a little. If you hit them often enough and hard enough, they didn't play as effectively. I wouldn't hesitate to go after someone for what appeared to be no good reason. But most of the time I had a reason, even if it was simply to get our crowd back into the game.

I did always try to be mindful of the score and the situation when I was playing really aggressively. I didn't want to poke a sleeping giant and get him riled up. I picked my spots. You have to target opponents at the right time if your objective is to provide a spark for your team. Sometimes my timing wasn't perfect, but I believed the good outweighed the bad on most nights.

Plus, I knew my coach wasn't going to bench or punish me if I skated off the straight and narrow from time to time. Keenan didn't want me to err on the side of caution when it came to physical play.

In my last full season in Montreal, I had 185 penalty minutes. In my first four seasons in Chicago, my penalty minute totals rose to 192, 245, 282, and 212.

Intimidation was such an important part of Keenan's strategy that he came in one day and ordered us to wear these huge Donzis-brand shoulder pads. He believed they made us look bigger and more intimidating than we were, but we felt like they made us look like Robocops. Apparently, he had convinced players to wear them in Philadelphia when he coached there, but most of our guys wouldn't wear them. You could barely move in those things.

To me, it seemed as if he treated us worse when we were winning than he did when we were losing.

KEENAN HAD TO WORK to find reasons to be mad at us in 1990–91 because the Blackhawks posted a 49–23–8 record and captured the Presidents' Trophy as the NHL's top regular season team. We only gave up 211 goals that season; no other NHL team gave up fewer than 249 goals.

We were a tough, skilled, physical team that lived and died by the sword.

Unfortunately, we got cut in the opening round of the playoffs.

The Minnesota North Stars were 27–39–14 in the regular season, but they scored a crazy number of power play goals against us and upset us in six games.

Undisciplined to a fault, we allowed the North Stars to tie the NHL record with 15 power play goals in the series.

We led the best-of-seven series 2–1 going into Game 4. We fought with the North Stars before the puck was dropped to start the game. The two teams combined for 139 penalty minutes and we lost 3–1. That contest was the turning point of the series. Keenan was so angry that on the flight home from Minnesota, he wouldn't let us have any food.

I had targeted Minnesota's Brian Bellows that night, who had at least one point in every game in the series. I was assessed a gross misconduct for eye-gouging him. What I was actually doing was trying to rip the toupee off his head.

There was some speculation that I might face a suspension that would begin at the start of the next season. But NHL vice president Brian O'Neill called me to Montreal for a hearing and then fined me $500 with no suspension.

Minnesota general manager Bob Clarke was incensed over what he considered a slap on the wrist.

That criticism was funny, considering that Clarke was known in his era for playing a similar style to mine. Clarke slashed Soviet star Alexander Kharlamov and broke his ankle at the 1972 Summit Series. Clarke's objective was to take Kharlamov out of the series.

Is that any different than what I was doing 20 years later?

Clarke and I weren't the only players in our eras that would attempt to take someone out of the lineup with a well-placed slash or hit.

In Game 5, the North Stars scored five power play goals and beat us 6–0, and our fans littered the Chicago Stadium ice with crushed paper cups.

Always looking to send a message, Keenan told the media after the game that the NHL was conspiring against us. His mind games didn't help. We were knocked out 3–1 in Game 6 in Minnesota. It didn't make us feel any better that the North Stars advanced all the way to the Stanley Cup Final, where they lost to the Pittsburgh Penguins.

Our goal had been to bring the Cup back to Chicago, and we failed.

YOU WOULD NEED AN army of psychologists to explain our team's relationship with Keenan. You were never sure what would happen with him next or exactly where you stood in his estimation.

He was an old-school coach who liked his players to hang out and drink together. He wanted his players to bond and to stick together on and off the ice. At practice, he would ask which guys had been out late the night before. The players who hadn't gone out with the boys would be punished by having to skate extra hard.

Guys were always looking for ways to even the score with Keenan. Sometimes he would skate with us in practice, and I would slash him repeatedly.

We found a couple of new ways during a team trip to Banff, Alberta, when we got into Keenan's locker and lifted his team credit card out of his wallet. We used it to pay for a very expensive team dinner. It ended up being a few thousand dollars.

That night a few of us also came across Keenan in a drunken state and wrestled him down to the ground and gave him knuckle noogies.

Angry over the credit card incident, Keenan skated us for 45 minutes in practice the next day. But I was amused because Keenan was yelling at us with our black-and-blue knuckle marks all over his head.

A tough practice wasn't going to keep us from having fun in Banff. One of the things guys did there was sneak up to the hot springs to take a dip. Jeremy Roenick, Dale Tallon, and Dave Manson were the guys I remember being with me for some harmless fun. When we saw the police driving up the mountain, we fled downhill in various stages of undress.

Our teammate Mike Hudson had been momentarily detained by police. When he heard the police say on the radio that people were up at the springs, he told them, "There go the Blackhawks."

Crazy moments involving Keenan were commonplace in that era. One time, Keenan made Greg Gilbert a healthy scratch, even though Gilbert was a guy he liked. Gilbert's wife was so angry she came down to the dressing room to confront the coaches. I think she wanted to tear off Keenan's head, an impulse that plenty of boys in the room had from time to time. The coaches all hid in their offices as Mrs. Gilbert stewed outside.

We had several memorable moments with Keenan at the Lodge Bar. The coaches and players both liked that place. The rule was that if the players were there first, then the coaches had to drink elsewhere. If Keenan was there first, then we had to find another watering hole. Those were the house rules.

Keenan liked to drink but he wasn't a particularly good drinker. To his credit, you could tell him to kiss your ass when he was drinking and he wouldn't hold it against you later.

When Brett Hull was playing for the St. Louis Blues, he was in the Lodge with me one night when Keenan walked in, already looking like he'd had a drink or two.

Keenan marched straight up to Hullie, who was standing at the bar.

"You couldn't play for me," he blurted out as if he was revealing the meaning of life.

"Wouldn't want to," Hullie said.

Hullie's reply had everyone in stitches. Even Keenan laughed.

Then I told Keenan to hit the road.

"Rules are rules," I said.

Life in the Blackhawks dressing room was never dull. At one point, the late comedian Chris Farley got interested in the team and started coming to our games. Once, he came into our dressing room, climbed on a stationary bike, and started pedaling as hard as he could. He had everyone cracking up.

Blackhawks forwards Bernie Nicholls and Joe Murphy lived in the same building as Farley, and believe it or not, many of us were out with him the night before he died about a week before Christmas in 1997. We ate at Gibson's Bar and Steakhouse and then went over to Stanley's Kitchen and Tap. Chris was drinking vodka, heavily.

A few of us told him he needed to be careful with his drinking. "I know," he said.

He was gone for a second and then returned with a joint hanging out of his mouth. We could tell that Farley was living his life dangerously.

I also hung out often with Michael Jordan and Dennis Rodman in Chicago. MJ liked having Rodman around because it took the pressure off of him when they were out in public. Everyone always flocked toward Rodman because you never knew what he might do next.

Rodman had four seats reserved under the basket for his guests, and fans always looked forward to see who Rodman had invited. It might be model Cindy Crawford, or Pearl Jam's Eddie Vedder, or some transvestites that Rodman knew, or a couple of the Blackhawks.

Rodman cut a deal with an entertainment production company and was given free use of a party bus in exchange for the right to film anything that happened when he arrived at his destination. He would go to strip clubs, bars, and anywhere else where he could find the nightlife. I would board his bus occasionally, but I wouldn't show my face until the cameras had followed him inside the establishment.

In 1998, after our season was over, Brian Noonan and I flew to Salt Lake City to watch Jordan, Rodman, and the Chicago Bulls play Game 5 of the NBA Finals against the Utah Jazz. The Bulls lost, but Rodman had a van waiting to take us to the airport for what was intended to be a quick trip to Las Vegas.

After Noonan and I had been sitting in the van for a while waiting for Rodman to come out, he emerged from the arena with Bulls coach Phil Jackson in hot pursuit. Phil was about 20 paces behind and closing quickly.

"Dennis, are you going to be at practice tomorrow?" Phil asked.

"Yep," Rodman said.

Noonan and I were doing our best to hide because we didn't want Phil to know we were accessories to Rodman's crime.

"Are you sure, Dennis?" Phil asked. "I know you are going somewhere. Can we count on you?"

"Yep, we're cool," Rodman said.

As the van pulled away, I heard Phil say, "I see you in there, Chelios."

Shocker: Rodman didn't make it to practice the next day. In fact, we had to drag him out of his room at 10:00 in the morning.

The Bulls won their sixth title of the Jordan era in Game 6 on MJ's dramatic, now-famous final shot. Rodman was out to lunch for the first two quarters, but he scored seven points and played his usual tough defense.

One time the Bulls and Blackhawks played back-to-back games in Vancouver, and we convinced players from both teams to all go out together at Roxy's. Even straitlaced Bull Steve Kerr was there. I remember Jeremy Roenick was shooting pool with Jordan. Everyone in the bar was watching us. It was a great night.

That was before the age of iPhones, Instagram, and Twitter, meaning we were allowed to have a good time without incriminating photos and stories all over the Internet.

We stayed at the bar until about 6:00 AM, which was when the Blackhawks had to leave for the airport. The Bulls were shellacked by the Vancouver Grizzlies the next night, and forward Scottie Pippen ratted us out to the media.

"We were out with the Hawks all night," Pippen said in defense of the Bulls' dismal performance.

Reading that nugget in the Chicago newspapers, our coach Darryl Sutter punished us the next day by skating us for 45 minutes with no pucks involved. Thanks, Scottie!

IN 1991–92, WE PLAYED with more discipline than usual, at least during the playoffs. We had won 11 consecutive postseason games and put the Blackhawks in the Stanley Cup Final for the first time since 1973. We believed we were going to take down the defending Stanley Cup champion Pittsburgh Penguins. The Penguins had guys like Mario Lemieux, Ron Francis, Jaromir Jagr, Bryan Trottier, Kevin Stevens, and Rick Tocchet, among others. We thought we could take them.

Didn't happen.

In Game 1, we had leads of 3–0 and 4–1 but ended up losing 5-4, with a young Jagr scoring a career-making tying goal late in the game. I think Brent Sutter, our best defensive forward, was turned around three times on Jagr's incredible drive to the net. Most people don't remember the replays that showed a Penguin was holding one of our defensemen's stick. But it was a great goal by Jagr. Lemieux won the game on a power play goal with 13 seconds left in regulation. It was a devastating loss for our team.

To me, however, the turning point of the series was Game 2, when Keenan benched the line of Steve Larmer, Jeremy Roenick, and Michel Goulet. That is when I believe we lost the series.

Roenick was one of my best friends on the Blackhawks. We ran hard together, especially when we were on the road. At home, Roenick spent much of his time with his wife and with several friends he had that existed outside the world of hockey. I had no friends outside of hockey back then. But away from Chicago, Roenick was the life of the party. He could sing, he could dance, and he could score goals. The man knows the words to every song ever written and he could find a seam in any defense. He was a feisty, competitive center.

It was impossible for me to believe that benching Roenick's line at that point in the series was a good idea.

I remember assistant coach Darryl Sutter sitting in the back of the plane trying to convince us that Keenan was justified in his decision, but I wouldn't drink that Kool-Aid. Darryl was a company man who was just backing our coach.

Whenever our team fell behind, it seemed like Keenan would start making bizarre moves, like benching our top scoring line. To me, that was like quitting. It was one of the aspects of his coaching style I found frustrating.

Keenan was scrambling after that loss to explain why he had benched his scorers. Roenick had been slashed in that game by Pittsburgh's Kevin Stevens, which had resulted in a bad bruise. But Keenan made Roenick wear a cast on his hand to suggest he had suffered a far more serious injury.

At his press conference, Keenan made it clear that he was sending a message to officials that they were missing penalty calls. But the media saw through Keenan's theatrics and presumed he was just looking for some defense for benching Roenick, Larmer, and Goulet.

I believe we could have won that series against Pittsburgh. However, after what happened in Game 2, I think we lost our swagger. We got swept instead.

THE UNFORTUNATE TRUTH OF my enjoyable days with the Blackhawks is that after 1992 we never really threatened to win the Stanley Cup again.

In 1992, Bill Wirtz made Keenan choose between being the general manager or the coach. Keenan chose to be GM, and then Wirtz fired him a few months later anyway.

Darryl Sutter was promoted to be our new coach, and he was a Keenan clone. We won 47 games in 1992–93 and I won my second Norris Trophy. But the joy of that season was washed away after we were swept by the St. Louis Blues in the opening round of the playoffs.

We also lost in the first round of the playoffs in 1993–94, that time to Toronto.

During the lockout-shortened 1994–95 season, we had a mediocre 24–19–5 record and yet made it to the Western Conference Final. We had swept the Vancouver Canucks in the second round, and I had two overtime game-winners in that series. Those may have been my two most important goals as a Hawk. They came in Games 3 and 4 in a series that was actually much tighter than a sweep would indicate.

While many Chicago fans remember those back-to-back overtime goals, the truth is that I probably played better defensively than I did offensively in that series.

My assignment was to stop the dynamic Pavel Bure, who had scored seven goals during Vancouver's first-round win over the St. Louis Blues. He only had one assist against us before he left Game 4 in the second period with what was called a hip ligament pull.

Late in that season, Denis Savard had been traded back to the Blackhawks (by the Tampa Bay Lightning) and he assisted on my series-clinching goal. Funny how things turn out sometimes.

On that play, Dirk Graham was actually going to freeze the puck along the boards, but Savard saw the scoring opportunity developing and screamed at him to play it.

Graham kicked it up to Savard, who slipped past the defenseman and then sent a perfect pass to me as I skated through the middle.

It was our misfortune to be in the same conference as Detroit, because we were playing well before facing the Red Wings in the conference final. They beat us in five.

By 1995–96, Craig Hartsburg was our coach. He was a very nice guy, and we won 40 games. I won another Norris Trophy after leading the Blackhawks with 72 points. But again, we didn't go far enough in the playoffs, bowing out to the Colorado Avalanche in six games in the second round.

The loss to the Avalanche was particularly hard to take because I had missed a game after our team doctor, the late Dr. Louis Kolb, stuck a needle in the wrong place when he was attempting to freeze my groin before the game.

Dealing with a sports hernia, I wanted the area numbed long enough for me to get through the game. Before we hit the ice, Dr. Kolb gave me a shot. As soon as he left, our trainer Mike Gapski said he thought Dr. Kolb may have given me the shot in the wrong spot.

I wish our trainer would have spoken up beforehand. I could walk fine, but as soon as I got on the ice and pushed my leg to the side I fell down. I thought I had just hit a rut. But when I got up and tried again, back down I went. I realized quickly that I had no feeling in my leg when I tried to skate.

The Blackhawks announced that I had an equipment problem as I headed back to the dressing room and tried to figure out how to coax some feeling back into my leg. I rode the stationary bike. I climbed into the hot tub. Nothing worked.

In the *Chicago Tribune* the next day, columnist Bob Verdi called it the "longest equipment problem" in NHL history.

After each period, I tried to skate but simply couldn't get my leg to work. The freezing agent wouldn't wear off. The game went to overtime, but I was still numb. By the start of the third overtime, my leg had started to come around but I was still in no condition to skate.

Then Joe Sakic scored for the Avalanche on the 57th shot of the game against Ed Belfour to give the Avalanche a 3–2 win.

Shortly thereafter, the freezing agent wore off.

Obviously, missing that game bothered me greatly because the Avalanche had tied that best-of-seven series 2–2. Could I have made a difference in that game? We will never know, but at that time of my career I was playing a ton of minutes. I had played more than 30 in three different games in the first-round sweep against Calgary. If I had been on a shift during that third OT, could I have stopped Sakic from netting the game-winner?

Considering I had played on a cracked ankle during the playoffs the season before, it's a given that I could have been effective with my groin issue if my leg hadn't been numb.

The Avalanche ended up winning the Stanley Cup that season, sweeping the Florida Panthers. That needle being pushed in the wrong place on my leg could have cost us the Stanley Cup.

In 1996–97, we were below .500 for the first time in eight years and lost in the first round of playoffs. The following season we missed the playoffs and Hartsburg was fired.

In the press conference announcing Hartsburg's dismissal, general manager Bob Murray singled me out as a veteran who had failed Hartsburg. Murray said I had been "distracted" during the season.

It was written that Hartsburg and I didn't get along but that wasn't true. I liked and respected him. As Blackhawks captain, I had the right to challenge him on occasion. Good captains push back against their coaches. It was my job to represent the players' interests. Ultimately, coaches coach and players play. But most quality coaches seem to appreciate some give-and-take with their captains. That gives coaches a better grasp of what is happening in the dressing room.

When they named me captain, they had to know that I wasn't going to be a yes man. I always gave my coach the respect a guy in that position deserves, but I reserved the right to look at him funny if I believed one of his decisions was questionable.

What I can tell you is that no one felt worse about missing the playoffs that year than me. I had been named captain in 1995, and I took that responsibility seriously.

Despite what Murray had said about me, my focus was completely on what we needed to do to push the Blackhawks back into the playoffs.

I was a Chicago native and I loved being a Blackhawk. I didn't want to go my entire career without helping the Blackhawks win a Stanley Cup. My contract with the Blackhawks was scheduled to expire in 2000. I asked my agents, Tom and Steve Reich, to talk to the organization about extending it.

My assumption was that I was going to play several more seasons for the Blackhawks and then stay with the organization in some capacity after I retired.

What I didn't know was that the Blackhawks organization didn't share my vision for the future.

8

I Never Wanted to Leave

The first indication that the Chicago Blackhawks didn't want me anymore was when new coach Dirk Graham told me early in the 1998–99 season that he didn't want my children in the dressing room.

Everyone in the organization knew that I enjoyed bringing my kids to the rink, but Graham walked right up to me and said he wasn't going to allow them to hang around anymore.

As team captain, I protested, noting that players liked to bring their kids in. Obviously professional athletes travel a lot, and having our kids around during practices and off days provides us an opportunity to make up for those absences in a way that is fun for them, too.

"Dirk," I said, "you can't just say, 'No kids.'"

He backed off and agreed to set aside certain days that kids would be allowed in the dressing room. That seemed like a fair compromise.

To me, the issue seemed resolved until I brought my son Jake to the rink to skate at 8:00 in morning. That was a full four hours before we were scheduled to practice.

It was a day when kids weren't supposed to be in the dressing room, so I hustled him out before the guys started showing up. I told him to hang out in trainer Lou Varga's laundry room.

My mistake was leaving Jake's hockey bag by my stall. Graham saw the bag and asked someone who it belonged to. When he was told that my son was watching television in Louie's room, he was pissed.

I was getting dressed for practice when Dirk summoned me.

"Take your gear off and go home," he said.

"What?" I said.

"You directly violated my rules," he said.

I pointed out that he had brought his two daughters in on a day they weren't allowed. He explained that he had happened to have his girls that day and decided to bring them in.

Realizing I wasn't going to get anywhere with logic, I said, "Dirk, just fine me, and I will pay it. Don't embarrass me in front of my teammates."

"No, I've made my decision," he said.

I reminded him that when we had played together, we always had our children around. That's one of the reasons it was fun to play for the Blackhawks.

"Are you arguing with me?" Graham asked.

Then he got up and acted as if he wanted to fight.

"Dirk, I'm not going to fight you," I said. "C'mon."

"I want you to go home," Graham said.

"What are you going to tell the players?" I asked.

"Leave that up to me."

I went back out, took my gear, and left.

After that incident, Graham started to make me miserable whenever the opportunity arose. There were times when I was nursing an injury and felt like I shouldn't be in the lineup, but somehow I'd find myself being put back out on the ice. The last thing I ever wanted to do was let my teammates down, so I'd go out there and do the best I could.

Once he put me at center on a line with Bob Probert and Reid Simpson on my wings against the Colorado Avalanche. We lined up against Joe Sakic's line. Sakic looked up and me and asked, "What are you doing here?"

"I don't think I'm going to be here much longer—can you let me win the faceoff?" I asked.

He laughed.

That was probably the most difficult period in my career, because I truly believed I was going to retire as a Blackhawk. That is all I wanted. My parents had moved back to Chicago. I had overwhelming respect for owner Bill Wirtz. Chicago was my hometown. I grew up watching Bobby Hull and Stan Mikita. I rooted for the Cubs, the Bears, and the Bulls. I considered Michael Jordan a close friend. Following in my father's footsteps, I owned a restaurant in Chicago named Cheli's Chili Bar. At that point, the idea of playing anywhere but Chicago had zero appeal to me.

As is often the case in relationships between players and the teams they play for, money was a complicating factor.

The previous summer, my agents had asked the Blackhawks about a contract extension but general manager Bob Murray said he wasn't interested.

My timing wasn't great. In 1997–98, the Blackhawks had just missed the playoffs for the first time since 1969.

After the season, Murray pointed a finger at me, implying that my failed leadership and my subpar season (three goals, 39 assists, minus-7) had played a significant role in the Blackhawks' fall in the standings.

The 1998–99 season didn't go any better. Just after Thanks-giving, we owned a record of 5–14–3. It looked as if we would miss the playoffs for a second consecutive season.

When Graham and I were teammates, we had always been friendly to each other. I respected Graham as a player and leader. I believe strongly that you don't have to be a star player to be a captain, and I always hold up Graham as an example of that. He wasn't a superstar, but you could count on him playing well in important games.

I spent most of the 1998–99 season begging Graham to explain why he was treating me like a leper. We had stood shoul-der to shoulder as teammates, but now he was acting as if he didn't want me in his dressing room.

"If I'm going to put up with this, I want some stability," I said.

During that season, there were constant whispers, rumors, and speculation that I would be traded.

On January 17, the *New York Post* published a report that said Wirtz and I had an agreement that I would be traded if the team wasn't in contention later in the season.

"I swear on my kids' heads that that's not true at all," I told the Chicago media. "I have no interest in being traded anywhere."

That was the truth. At that point, I could not imagine playing anywhere except Chicago.

"As bad as things are right now, I want to be here when this thing turns around and to lead the charge," I added. "I want to stay in Chicago. I don't know how I can put it simpler. Things are going bad here, but I'm not the type of player who is going to quit or ask to be traded. My heart is in Chicago and it's always going to be in Chicago."

What the media didn't know—and something that I didn't tell them—was that I had a handshake no-trade agreement with Mr. Wirtz. He told me he would not trade me during the duration of the contract.

My situation changed in February when Murray told the *Chicago Tribune* that my existing contract was negotiated under the belief that it would be "my last contract with the Hawks."

Seeing that in print stunned both me and my agents.

Although Murray hedged and said he might reconsider if I played well in 2000, he made it sound as if that was a long shot rather than a realistic possibility.

It wasn't as if I was playing poorly. I was playing 27 minutes per game for the NHL's third-worst defensive team, and I was minus-4.

Just three years before I had won the Norris Trophy as the NHL's best defenseman. Only two years before, I was a second-team NHL All-Star, meaning I was considered among the NHL's top four defensemen.

Even if the organization wanted to go in a different direction, couldn't the Blackhawks have treated me with more respect near the end of my time?

As Steve Reich pointed out publicly, this wasn't how the Bruins were dealing with Raymond Bourque, who was only a couple of years older than me.

On February 22, Graham was fired as the head coach, and assistant Lorne Molleken was promoted to coach on an interim basis. It didn't seem like that changed how Murray perceived my future with the organization.

Six days before the trade deadline, I heard that Bob Probert and Dave Manson were going to be placed on waivers. It seemed like a fire sale was imminent, and the Blackhawks were going to embrace a traditional rebuilding effort. It looked as if they were going to strip the roster down to the bare bones and go with younger players.

Immediately, I dialed Mr. Wirtz's lawyer and left a message saying that I wanted to talk about a contract extension. When he didn't return my call, I figured his answer couldn't be any clearer. It was obvious that Murray and the Blackhawks had decided that I wasn't going to lead the rebuilding effort.

Murray told me to just play out my contract and then there would be a job for me within the organization. I knew that if Murray said that, he did so with the blessing of Mr. Wirtz. If Mr. Wirtz said I would have a job, I would have a job.

The problem was that I didn't feel as if I was at the end of my career—far from it. I felt like I had some gas left in the tank, and the thought of hanging up my skates forever just because the front office wanted me to didn't feel right.

For a couple of days, I did consider the possibility that my career was over, but after a lot of soul searching I told Murray to trade me. It was one of the hardest decisions I ever had to make. I would've done almost anything to finish my career in Chicago; I just wanted to do it on my terms.

"I don't care where I go," I told Murray. "Just trade me. I won't argue about where you send me."

To their credit, the Hawks granted me and my agents the right to negotiate with other teams. The San Jose Sharks and Philadelphia Flyers were the teams most interested in me, and the Carolina Hurricanes were also in the mix.

Then suddenly, Detroit general manager Ken Holland came out of nowhere with an offer.

The Red Wings were trying to win their third consecutive Stanley Cup, and they had been searching two years for a defenseman to replace Vladimir Konstantinov, who couldn't play after suffering brain damage in a 1997 limousine accident. The Red Wings were willing to give me a two-year extension for $11 million. The $5.5 million per season represented a significant raise.

In compensation to the Blackhawks, they offered a younger defenseman, Anders Eriksson, and two first-round draft picks. The Red Wings were giving me the kind of respect that I had been looking for from the Blackhawks. Clearly, they didn't think I was washed up just yet.

So much has been made of me going to play for the Red Wings, but ironically, one of the biggest reasons I decided to go to Detroit was because it was so close to Chicago. You could make the drive between the two cities in under five hours. The flight time was less than an hour. It would be so much easier on my family than trying to relocate to one of the coasts.

Also, my sister Gigi had been battling cancer for a long time, and I wanted to be close enough to travel home to see her. She had been fighting off the disease for almost a decade, going into remission twice. But now the cancer had returned, and I didn't want to be too far away from her. We were only a year and half apart in age and we were very close.

I had just built a new, beautiful home in Chicago, and I told my wife we would not be selling it because I expected to return home. My plan was to rent it.

Even though I was fully aware of what was happening behind the scenes, when the trade actually went through I felt like I'd been punched in the gut.

Once it was announced, the first person I tried to call was Mr. Wirtz, because I wanted to tell him how much I appreciated playing for his team. He always lived up to his word with me.

My fondness for Mr. Wirtz can't be overstated. I respected him as a businessman and for the passion he had for his team.

Mr. Wirtz was a tough negotiator. He used to say, "I *could* pay you that amount. But I *won't* pay you that amount."

He would laugh, and I would laugh. I loved the man.

His handshake was more binding than any contract. Behind the scenes, Mr. Wirtz helped people and never let anyone know about it.

He was proud to be the owner of the Blackhawks, and he believed players should be proud to wear that jersey. I know I felt that way, and I was proud to play for him.

Family is the most important aspect of my life. I can tell you that Mr. Wirtz was absolutely adored and loved by his children. I think that says more about him than anything else he ever did.

What the Blackhawks told me was that Wirtz "wasn't available by phone." I wasn't sure what that meant. Did he not want to talk to me?

Eventually I was able to get in touch with him and I made it clear to him that I appreciated how he had treated me. When I left Chicago, I left on good terms with Mr. Wirtz. I fully believed that I would be coming back home and working in the Hawks organization when I was done playing.

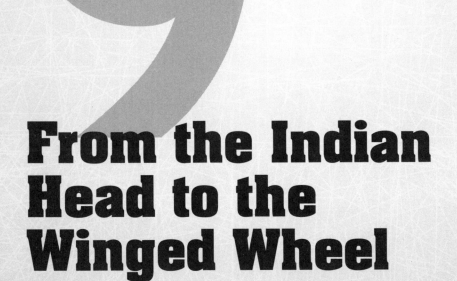

From the Indian Head to the Winged Wheel

had famously said once in a television interview that I would "never" play for the Detroit Red Wings.

I meant it when I said it. That's how deep the rivalry was between the Blackhawks and the Red Wings.

When I settled into my hotel room after being traded to Detroit, that interview was being played on the local news. I'm sure it was played over and over in Chicago. Blackhawks fans remember that interview and never forgave me for agreeing to play for the Red Wings.

I'm not sure I can really blame them.

In my defense, it was not easy for me to walk into Detroit's dressing room for the first time. It was like crossing enemy lines. I had tussled with Red Wings captain Steve Yzerman a few times during my career, and Sergei Fedorov had been a frequent target of mine. A few years before, the NHL had fined me $500 for slashing him.

"I used to do everything to Sergei," I told *Sports Illustrated* writer Michael Farber. "Those were the days when you could elbow a guy and not worry about getting suspended. I took advantage of that."

Farber pointed out in his story that I had previously been "hanged in effigy" by some fans at Joe Louis Arena.

The first time I dressed to play for the Red Wings, I had to do it twice because I had forgotten to remove my gym shorts the first time. Then, I mistakenly put on my elbow pads before my shoulder pads. To say I was out of sorts would be an understatement.

My presence in the dressing room was also odd for my new teammates, many of whom had fought me like gladiators through the years. It was pretty awkward for all of us.

On my first day, tough guy Darren McCarty picked up one of my sticks and said, "This is the first time I've ever been this close to one of these without it being broken over my head."

On my second day in Detroit, rugged Red Wings forward Marty Lapointe came up to me and asked, "Are we going to be okay?"

I just laughed. I think he believed we should apologize to each other for all of the bad blood we'd built up over the years.

The one player I did apologize to was center Kris Draper. I had said some mean things to him in the past. After he was hurt by that Claude Lemieux hit from behind in 1996, his mother threatened to file a lawsuit against Lemieux. Not long after, Draper and I were both stretching before one of our games, and I leaned over and called him a pussy and suggested he tell his mother to stay out of it.

I had also uttered stupid comments to defenseman Larry Murphy about dyeing his hair that I regretted saying. I don't recall whether I apologized to Murph about those comments, but I should have. In the heat of battle, you say dumb things. Now, Murphy and I are great friends.

There was a buzz in Detroit about the Red Wings at that time, and not just because I was now playing for the team. Holland had also acquired goalie Bill Ranford, defenseman Ulf Samuelsson, and feisty scoring winger Wendel Clark. All the players were on the ice 15 minutes early for the first practice with the new group.

The Red Wings were now considered the team to beat for the Stanley Cup. After the roster makeover, Las Vegas oddsmakers were now making us a 2–1 favorite, down from 6–1.

According to news reports, the Red Wings sold 171 jerseys with my name or Clark's name on the back the day after the trades were announced.

Many fans in Detroit came up to me and said, "We used to hate you but now we love you."

The Red Wings used the "left wing lock" defensive system at the time, and that was less taxing on defensemen. As a right-side defenseman, I no longer had to make the long diagonal skate to the left corner to get the puck on an opponent's dump-in. The left wing had the responsibility of retrieving the puck in those instances.

Legendary head coach Scotty Bowman had the Wings playing a puck-possession game, so I had more freedom to join the rush under his command. In fact, I was supposed to jump into the play on certain breakouts, and I forgot a couple of times in my first few games. In Chicago we moved the puck from defenseman to defenseman and then fired it up the boards.

My minutes were trimmed in Detroit, but in a good way. In my last three games in Chicago, I had averaged more than 30 minutes per game. In my first three games in Detroit, I averaged just under 25 minutes per game.

The first time I stepped on the ice for a warm-up in a Red Wings jersey, the fans stood and applauded. Apparently they were quick to forgive and forget.

Truthfully, I was pretty pleased to be joining a team that had an established captain such as Steve Yzerman. Given what I had just gone through in Chicago, I was happy to just concentrate on hockey and not dressing room politics.

Yzerman was an intimidating presence, even among the veteran players. If we lost a game, there wasn't a guy in the room who would make eye contact with Yzerman. Even at my age, I had a healthy fear of him.

Once, in front of the entire team, Yzerman called me out after Paul Kariya had scored an overtime goal to beat us. On the play, I had left Kariya alone to try and help Yzerman.

"Stay with your fucking guy," Yzerman told me.

I didn't much like how he opted to bring that to my attention. I had always made it a point never to embarrass a teammate.

The next day I told Yzerman how I felt about his approach.

"If you don't like what I'm doing, just pull me aside and talk to me about it," I said.

To Yzerman's credit, he did apologize. But I respected how much he cared about how the team played. He was a great captain and a great player. He just wanted me to do my job. I understood that.

And I loved playing for Scotty Bowman. I liked how he used me, and he didn't treat me as if he believed I was at the end of my career.

From my time in Montreal, I know the Scotty who coached me wasn't the same Scotty who coached the Canadiens in the 1970s. The guys who played for Scotty then considered him the toughest, meanest SOB they'd ever met.

"But you won five Stanley Cup with Scotty," I said once to Hall of Famer Larry Robinson.

"Yeah, but we should have won 10," Robinson said.

Bowman clearly had softened by the time he landed in Detroit. He was quite a character. He would walk in and ask you a question but then wouldn't stay around to hear your answer. You'd be in mid-sentence and see him walking out the door. I guess he wasn't all that interested in what we had to say.

One time, he must have overheard a conversation about my Greek heritage or read about my father coming from Greece, because he walked up to me and said, "So you are an immigrant, eh?"

"Actually, I was born in the United States," I said. "You were born in Canada, so I think that makes *you* the immigrant."

I thought that was a snappy comeback, but Scotty didn't hear it because he was already back in his office by the time I opened my mouth.

I found Scotty quite entertaining, and he was awesome at handling our very talented team.

It wasn't Bowman's style to confront players individually. He made his points by the way he played guys or what he said to the entire group.

Early in my time in Detroit, Bowman was talking to us about our recent games, and he said he no longer wanted to see "any of that stuff after the whistles."

He never mentioned me by name, but he was clearly talking to me. From that point on, I didn't do anything like that in a Detroit jersey. I respected Scotty too much to defy him.

Although it was definitely strange to see myself on television highlights wearing a Red Wings jersey, I knew that eventually the feeling would pass and I could get back to just being a hockey player.

The worst night came on the last night of the regular season when I played my first game for the Red Wings in Chicago's United Center.

The fans booed me every time I touched the puck. I know I should have expected that reaction, but to be honest it was unnerving. That was when I realized the depth of anger the Chicago fans had worked up for me. They saw me as a traitor.

Bowman didn't put me on the ice much after the first period. Finally, he told me to leave the bench and go hang out with Michael Jordan, who had come to the game to see me.

"All you are doing is getting the crowd into the game," Scotty said.

Per Scotty's instructions, I dressed and watched the third period with Jordan in a suite. My old team wound up beating my new team 3–2.

Jordan had my back, telling everyone, "I'm not here for the Blackhawks. I'm here for Chris Chelios. I don't like how they treated him."

That was nice of MJ to say, but as I mentioned, I didn't have any ill will toward the Hawks.

My first Red Wings playoff experience didn't go much better for me than my Blackhawks regular season experience. It started well enough when we swept the Anaheim Ducks in the opening four, and then won the first two games of a second-round series against the Colorado Avalanche.

Riding a six-game winning streak, it looked as if we had a good chance to become the first team since the New York Islanders to win three Cups in a row (1980–83). But the Avalanche stunned us by beating us four in a row to knock us out of the playoffs. Just like that, it was over.

Then a strange thing happened. After the final team meeting, I returned to the hotel where I had been living since coming to Detroit. Given how fired up I was about my summer routine, I should have been out the door headed home in an hour's time.

Instead, I stayed in that hotel room for three straight days.

I had never known depression in my life until those three days. I was simply overwhelmed by what had happened over the previous few months. I was angry, sad, conflicted, listless, and lost. I lacked purpose. I didn't seem to know what to do next.

On the third day, Tracee called and asked, "Are you coming home?"

She snapped me back to reality. That's when I realized how upset I truly was about the trade. It was the start of a slow climb toward understanding how traumatic the move from Chicago to Detroit had been on my life.

If there was one misconception I wish I could have cleared up at that time, it was that moving from the Hawks to the Wings was easy for me. I think some people thought I didn't care which jersey I pulled on, that I just packed up my gear and went about my life like I had just changed a pair of socks. That couldn't have been further from the truth.

That summer was the worst summer of training I ever had during my NHL career. I didn't start to feel normal again until just before camp, after I had gotten my family settled in the Detroit area. Even then, I looked at Detroit as a temporary stop, just a place to pass through until I could return to Chicago. It seemed inevitable that I would be working for the Hawks organization when I was done playing.

As it turned out, neither Murray nor I was around for the Blackhawks' rebuilding effort, one that took much longer than anticipated. He was fired eight months after I left, with Bob Pulford returning to his former job as general manager. The Blackhawks only made one playoff appearance between 1998 and 2008.

Never in a million years would I have thought that I would play longer in Detroit than I played in Chicago.

Then again, who would have guessed that I would be 47 when I played my last game in Detroit in 2009? Nor would I have guessed that I would still be living in Detroit 16 years after the trade that changed my life.

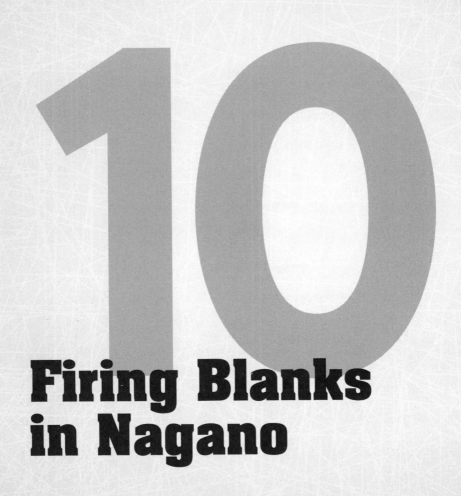

10

Firing Blanks in Nagano

On the morning the American hockey team was scheduled to leave the 1998 Olympic Games in Nagano, Japan, my U.S. teammate John LeClair pulled me aside to say he had fixed a "little problem" the boys had created the night before.

"The guys messed up the rooms a little bit," LeClair said. "But don't worry, I took care of it. I tipped the maids and it is all going to be taken care of."

By the time we arrived at the airport the vandalism was being treated in the media like a war crime. I blame the Canadian press for making it a much bigger event than it was. My theory is that Canada's poor performance at the Olympics had left Canadian reporters with nothing to write about. We were a target of opportunity.

The media was waiting for us in force when we arrived at the airport. It was a mob scene.

I had actually learned about the situation before LeClair told me. When teammate Gary Suter and I had returned to the Olympic Athletes Village the night before after being out with some members of the U.S. women's hockey team, we noticed that we were creating white footprints with each step we took as we got closer to our rooms.

"It's not snowing," I said. "What's going on?"

Then I thought, *Oh, no.*

Most of the players had already checked out. We determined quickly it was fire extinguisher foam that we were stepping in, and when I looked inside the rooms I knew there was likely to be trouble in the morning.

Unquestionably, it was stupid for the guys to mess up the rooms. It was an embarrassing situation. But these rooms were not damaged beyond repair. The initial estimate of damage was about $1,000, and as the story gained momentum in the press the estimated damage grew to $3,000.

My U.S. teammate Jeremy Roenick has always insisted that someone could have cleaned up the mess reasonably well with a regular old shop vac. Some of the damage to the chairs happened during the tournament because they were not designed to be used by heavy, big-bodied athletes. Some players simply sat down and the chairs disintegrated beneath them.

As captain, I had anticipated the potential for trouble after we lost our last game. This was two years after we had won the World Cup, and the Americans were considered one of the favorites to win the gold medal. Unfortunately, we played poorly in the Nagano tournament. After claiming a 2–1 lead in our first game against Sweden, we lost 4–2.

After taking care of Belarus 5–2, we then lost to Canada 4–1. The loss to Canada was stinging because it had only been 19 months since we had beaten that group in Montreal for the World Cup championship.

You don't want to believe this when you are a player, but anything can happen in a short tournament like the Olympics. When I look back on it, what I remember is that we simply never had a great game. Nothing went right for us. Nobody was playing at his best.

With the likes of Roenick, Mike Modano, Brett Hull, Keith Tkachuk, LeClair, and Bill Guerin, we should have been a dominant offensive team. LeClair was in the midst of scoring 50 or more NHL goals for three consecutive seasons, but he didn't score a goal in that tournament. That's not to single out LeClair; it is an illustration of how nothing went right for us.

We were outscored 14–9 in that tournament, and if you don't count the Belarus game, we were outscored 12–4 by the teams with NHL players (Canada, Sweden, and the Czechs).

Against Canada, we just couldn't cover anyone in front of our net. The Canadians scored four goals by parking in front of the crease. The puck would wind up in front and a split-second later it would be behind our goalie Mike Richter.

We were just flat, and I don't know why. Was it the wider European ice surface? I just don't know. When you look at the roster, we should have played better than we did.

Some minor issues had cropped up. Because we had won at the World Cup, our coach Ron Wilson gave us plenty of leeway, even going as far as asking us how we wanted to play.

Now, despite what I've described about a give-and-take between coaches and players, a hockey team still needs structure. Teams should be run like the military. Soldiers and players expect to be told what to do.

But that certainly had nothing to do with the fact that none of us were at our best.

Some members of the media speculated that we lost because we spent too much time partying in Nagano. But that simply wasn't true.

"I was in bed by 8:00 PM eight of the 10 nights I was here," Hull told the media. "It was ridiculous the amount of time I spent listening to my CD player and doing crossword puzzles on my bed because I was bored stiff."

Maybe that was our problem. Maybe we should have lit up Nagano.

"You know, we weren't exactly angels at the World Cup," Hull said.

Even after our poor start, we could have still won the tournament if we had played well in the medal round. But Dominik Hasek made 38 saves to spark the Czech Republic to a 4–1 win against us in the quarterfinals. The Czechs went on to win the gold medal, but we felt like we were beaten by a team that we should have defeated, no matter how well Hasek played.

The shame of it was that all of us had been excited about being at the Olympics. We wanted to be on the big stage. We wanted to play for our country. We wanted to kick the Canadians' asses again. We wanted the gold medal.

Before the tournament, Tkachuk said anything less than gold would be a disappointment.

"We thought we were going to be invincible, and maybe we were too high on our horses," Hull said.

LeClair said players were "embarrassed" that we were going home without a medal. And we were. We knew we were capable of playing much better than we did.

After the loss to the Czechs, the mood in our dressing room was ugly. Guys were frustrated, and after a loss hockey players will say things they regret.

Tkachuk was the angriest player. "This was the biggest waste of time ever," he said. "I hate to be negative, but this is disgusting."

I can tell you that Tkachuk, the son of a Boston-area fire-fighter, loved representing his country and he didn't mean those words quite like they sound in print.

Guys were frustrated and I suspected some of them might get out of hand that night.

Something needed to be said. I pulled aside Tkachuk, Roenick, and Guerin and said, "It's bad enough how we lost. Let's make sure no one does anything stupid tonight."

I still remember Tkachuk getting this sincere, serious look on his face and saying, "We would never. We would never."

Even though it's been 16 years since it happened, I'm still not going to say who was responsible. That's just not who I am. Teammates stick together. When it comes to something like this, you keep it in the dressing room.

But I can tell you that NHL commissioner Gary Bettman and former NHLPA executive director Bob Goodenow knew the entire story quickly, because one of my teammates provided details after the IOC threatened to ban us from Olympic competition for life if we didn't reveal who was responsible.

Despite the pressure, I made up my mind that no one on our team was going to discuss what happened publicly or admit to anything. As captain, I was going to apologize to everyone for the incident and personally cover any damages. We were going to stick together as a team. I put the word out and everyone clammed up. I still believe today it was the right thing to do.

I wrote a check for $3,000 to the Japanese Olympic Committee to cover the cost of fixing up the rooms.

In my apology, I called our actions "inexcusable."

"I want to take this opportunity to apologize to the people of Japan, the Japanese Olympic Committee, the USOC, and to all hockey fans throughout the world," I said. "Bitter frustration at our own level of play caused a few team members to vent their anger in a way which is not in the tradition of NHL/Olympic sportsmanship."

The only good memory I have of that mess is that Blackhawks owner Bill Wirtz was the one man who supported our decision to not name the players involved.

My apology was made one day after Mr. Wirtz blasted the continuing investigation and the increasing criticism we were receiving over the vandalism. He compared the NHL's inquiry to paranoid Captain Queeg's probe of the stolen strawberries in the 1954 movie *The Caine Mutiny*.

"They were eliminated from competition, which is the worst thing that can happen to a hockey player, and in their frustration, they broke some chairs," Wirtz wrote in a letter to Bettman and representatives of USA Hockey, the USOC, and the NHL Players Association.

Wirtz made it clear that he believed the investigation was essentially a witch hunt. The International Olympic Committee seemed to want to have someone burned at the stake over this.

"It seems like all you gentlemen are great fans of Jonathan Swift in that you use exaggeration for effect—like the Brobdingnagians and Lilliputians in *Gulliver's Travels*," wrote Wirtz. "This incident is not the Black Sox scandal, but merely a group of dedicated NHL players disgusted in themselves [because] they did not do better for their country at the Olympics."

He was right. And he wasn't done writing.

"Please take the ball bearings out of your hands and let's get on with our work," Wirtz said. "You do not have the power to grant partial immunity or haul these players in front of a grand jury, and you do not have the right to invade their dressing room. Instead of castigating these individuals, why don't you thank these young men for breaking their backs to compete in the Olympics and then come home to compete for the Stanley Cup?"

Wirtz said he would be proud to have any of us as his sons, including those who perpetrated the vandalism. He announced that he supported our decision not to single anyone out.

"We preach to our players that hockey is a team sport and that teams win championships, not individuals," Wirtz wrote in his letter. "It is only natural that players stick together. I would not respect them if they did not."

Say what you will about the way Wirtz ran his Blackhawks team, but he stood up for his players. Blackhawks Tony Amonte, Keith Carney, Gary Suter, and myself were on that U.S. team, and he had our backs. Fans were always mad at him because he wouldn't televise home games, but I found that you always knew where you stood with Mr. Wirtz.

He had old-school principles, and he and he didn't compromise those principles under any circumstances. I could relate to that approach.

Shortly thereafter, I received a personal check from Wirtz to reimburse me for the money I paid to cover the damages. The players responsible for the damages also gave me checks to cover it.

We got ourselves into an embarrassing mess, and somehow I ended up making a profit out of it.

11

Winning Is a Habit

W hen I brought Michael Jordan into the Detroit Red Wings' dressing room for the first time not long after I was traded to the team, he asked Scotty Bowman if he "needed to teach me how to win again."

Scotty just gave MJ an impish grin and let it go at that.

But MJ wasn't that far off base; I had lost a lot of games toward the end of my career in Chicago. Playing for the Red Wings was definitely a different experience, starting with the fact that the dressing room was a Hall of Fame class waiting to happen.

Steve Yzerman. Nick Lidstrom. Igor Larionov. Brendan Shanahan. Larry Murphy. Sergei Fedorov. All of those guys were on the Detroit roster when I arrived.

Later on, we added Dominik Hasek, Brett Hull, and Luc Robitaille. It was an embarrassment of riches.

Playing for the Red Wings was always fun because we were winning most of the time. Not counting my partial 1998–99 season (when we won the first nine games I played in), I was on the Detroit squad for nine full seasons, and we won 457 regular season games. That's an average of almost 51 wins per season. We also won 16 playoff series, and reached the Stanley Cup Final three times, winning the Cup twice.

Nobody asked me to be a leader in Detroit, because Yzerman provided the only leadership the team truly needed. The dressing room took care of itself. The Red Wings didn't face much adversity.

And if something did need to be said, Yzerman was the player who said it.

Yzerman may as well have been an assistant coach, because he held all of the guys accountable. As a player, you didn't want to let him down. You didn't want to do anything that would earn "that look" from him.

My respect for Yzerman was immense because I knew he had worked for everything he had achieved. He wasn't a great practice player. Drills didn't seem to come naturally to him. In fact, he would often do drills completely wrong. But you flat-out couldn't outwork him. When the Europeans would bring over new offensive moves that Yzerman hadn't seen, he would work on them in practice until he had mastered them.

It didn't bother me in the least to be in a dressing room where my leadership ability wasn't required. In fact, it was a relief. After going through what I had in Chicago, it was refreshing to just come to the rink every day and concentrate on what my job was on the ice. I didn't have to fret about who was or wasn't playing well, or deal with the coach about every team issue. That was Yzerman's job. My job was just to play defense, and maybe be a part-time team social director.

In Darren McCarty's book, *My Last Fight*, he said I was like the team concierge, because I was always looking after what the guys needed away from the arena. Being a good team player was always important to me. That's probably another trait I inherited from my dad. He loved being out with his friends. Everyone in the neighborhood loved him. Just as my dad was the glue that held the neighborhood together, I tried to always do what I could to keep everyone happy in the dressing room. I believed if we all spent time together, we would care about each other. If we cared about each other, we would play well together.

My Detroit teammates also liked that I would take care of the business details when we were out on the town. That came from my background in the restaurant business. For example, whenever we went out to eat, I was the one who made sure that the wait staff was taken care of properly. When the Detroit Red Wings left a restaurant, I wanted the employees of that establishment to feel as if we treated them well.

One unexpected adjustment I had to make when I moved to Detroit was getting used to drinking wine. I was and always will be a beer drinker. But Yzerman, Shanahan, and a few of the other guys drank wine, and when they went out for dinner they only ordered off the top shelf.

We would always just split the bill, and the tab seemed quite expensive to the guy who didn't enjoy wine. I started drinking it just to get my money's worth.

Then I realized that if I sipped wine with dinner the night before the game, it impacted how I played in the game. I wasn't as sharp. My senses seemed dulled. That was the end of the wine-drinking phase of my NHL career.

ONE OF THE HIGHLIGHTS of my time in Detroit was getting to play for Bowman. Watching how he dealt with each of us as individuals was endlessly entertaining. I always sensed that Bowman particularly enjoyed messing with Brendan Shanahan.

Shanahan was a Hall of Fame hockey player, a scorer with toughness and a willingness to stand up for his teammates. I was glad he was on my team. But Shanahan was also a calculating guy, always working an angle, and I don't mind saying that.

He was a world-class bullshitter, and didn't think twice about chasing down members of the media if he thought they had treated him unfairly. He was always concerned about his image.

After we won Game 3 against Carolina in the 2002 Stanley Cup Final—a 3–2 triple-overtime thriller—I heard him whining about the game story that appeared in the next day's newspaper. I've never seen a guy just two wins away from a championship so depressed. I told him to shut up and worry about playing well.

Scotty pushed Shanahan's buttons every chance he had. If he had a message to deliver, Scotty didn't worry about ruffling a guy's feathers.

We never knew what we were going to get from Bowman on a daily basis. He possessed a radar-like ability that allowed him to see everything and a computer-like mind that allowed him to process many different factors at the same time. But during one game, he seemed distracted at the start. For the first six or eight minutes, he wasn't on top of everything the way he normally was.

Then out of the blue, he said to no one in particular, "Who is sitting in my seats?"

Bowman had his own set of personal tickets and had noticed that someone he didn't recognize was sitting in those seats. It bothered him enough that it threw him off his game. You can bet that between periods he dispatched a Red Wings employee to find out what was going on. That was how Scotty operated.

One time during the morning skate before a playoff game he noticed a television camera hanging from the scoreboard. He said it was too low, according to the league rules. He noted that we sometimes cleared the puck out of our zone by lofting the puck high into the air, and he feared that one of those clearing attempts was going to hit the camera and give our opponent an advantage.

As it turned out, he was right. The camera was too low.

On another game day, he decreed that there were too many rotating cameras around the rink and he had them removed.

A lot of people think of Bowman as a yeller, but the truth is he barely talked to us. He just didn't talk to the players very often… except for Brett Hull.

Almost every day Brett would grab a coffee and go sit in Scotty's office and shoot the breeze. If any other guy would have been in there, you would have suspected he was trying to get on Scotty's good side with the hope of earning more playing time. But honestly, no other player would have felt comfortable going into Scotty's office other than Brett.

Talk about an odd couple. But for some reason, everyone could see those two just hit it off. They would talk about a wide array of topics, and usually none of those topics included hockey. They would talk about golf or baseball or places they had been or Brett's dad, Bobby.

Guys would walk by and see Brett in there chatting away with Scotty and they'd just shake their heads.

Never could you be sure what Scotty was going to say next. When I first arrived in Detroit, I was appalled to discover that the Red Wings' sauna was small and out of date. Frankly, it was disgusting. It was tiny and less than inviting.

That wasn't going to work for me, because I believed in the power of sweating. I found a construction worker to come in and build a new one, large enough to hold eight people.

The new one included a big-screen television so I could ride the stationary bike in there without getting bored.

Riding a bike in the sauna was the one training habit that my teammates were always fascinated by. But I've always felt the sweating was good for you. I feel the same way today. I picked up the idea of riding the bike in the sauna from football coach Dave McClain while I was playing at Wisconsin. The irony of that is that McClain actually passed away in the sauna after riding a stationary bike.

But I've been doing it for more than 30 years and I found it is an effective way to manage my weight on days after I had too much to drink or eat.

Many of my teammates tried it and hated it. Many have called me crazy for doing it. But it works for me.

Right in the middle of the project, Scotty came over and asked what I was doing.

"Building a new sauna with a TV," I said. I swallowed hard, having no idea how this news was going to be received.

"I like it," Scotty said, and just walked away.

You never knew what you might find in our dressing room. We had a veteran group, and the guys had a lot of different interests that I didn't see in Chicago. For example, crossword puzzles were very popular in the Detroit dressing room. Hull was one of the kingpins of that pursuit. I didn't do crossword puzzles, but I told everyone the story I heard about how defenseman Denis Potvin was considered the best crossword guy on the New York Islanders for several years.

He was able to complete them amazingly fast. Then one day one of his teammates happened to pick up one of the crosswords that Potvin had completed and reported that Potvin didn't have any of the words right.

Whether it is true or not, I have no idea. But it is a funny story.

Joey Kocur, one of the toughest players in NHL history, was supposedly the best crossword guy in Detroit when I arrived. Then again, no one ever dared to check his work either.

I became close to Nicklas Lidstrom, and I loved Tomas Holmstrom. I don't think Tomas had any idea how funny he truly was.

But my best friend on the Red Wings was Brett. We rode to the rink together, and I always found him a very funny guy. Hull liked to complain and he liked to argue, and that was the source of much of his humor. Even if he was wrong about an issue, he could twist a debate around to the point where you couldn't remember what his original opinion was. He is an entertaining personality.

He and I went all the way back to the beginning of our careers. One of our first meetings came when I was playing for Montreal and Hullie was with the Flames. We were actually paired up during a big brawl in Calgary. We were really just talking when Brett's teammate Paul Baxter skated by and sucker-punched me.

"Go get him," Hull said, laughing.

So I did. I chased Baxter around the ice and got lucky because he fell down. I landed on top of him and started hammering away. Then Tim Hunter sucker-punched me from behind and it was all over.

When Hullie was in St. Louis, I tried to hurt him repeatedly during the playoffs. I would leave him alone in the regular season, but I made several attempts to break his wrist or hand in the playoffs.

He always assumed that I was acting on Mike Keenan's orders; the reality is that's just how I played once the playoffs started.

UNQUESTIONABLY, THE BEST DETROIT team I was on was the 2001–02 version that had the roster full of potential Hall of Famers. We were 51–17–10 that season, and won the Presidents' Trophy as the NHL's No. 1 team.

In the playoffs, we lost our first two games at home against Vancouver and got booed off the ice. With the team we had, it would have been ridiculous to be knocked out in the first round. We ended up winning the next four games against the Canucks. To be honest, once we had won Game 3 of that series, I was confident we were going to win the Stanley Cup.

Even when we lost the first game of the Final against Carolina at home, I just felt as if we were the better team and were going to win the series.

The turning point of that Final was a triple-overtime Game 3 that we won in Raleigh on Igor Larionov's goal. If Carolina had won that game, I suppose it could have been a different series. I had been around the game long enough to realize that anything could happen, and it's not easy to determine sometimes why teams win or lose. But I just felt as if we were in control. We had so many guys who could score.

On a personal note, I felt good about the contribution I'd made to the team. I played well that entire season. I was voted to the All-Star squad and I was runner-up to Nicklas Lidstrom in the Norris Trophy voting. In the playoffs, only Yzerman and Sergei

Fedorov had more assists than I had. Only Lidstrom played more than I was playing. Counting the overtime games we had, I averaged better than 26 minutes per game in the postseason. Not bad for a guy who had recently turned 40 years old.

During the season, Detroit native and rock star Kid Rock, whose real name is Bobby Ritchie, had told me that if we won the Stanley Cup he would throw us a party to end all parties.

The night we won the Stanley Cup at Joe Louis Arena, I dialed him up and said, "You owe us a party."

"And I will give you one," he said.

Kid and I were close friends, and we remain tight today. After I came to Detroit, I went to a Super Bowl party at Darren McCarty's home and he introduced us. It wasn't a surprise to meet a noted rocker at McCarty's place because McCarty knew everyone in town.

As fate would have it, Kid Rock had a concert scheduled in Madison, Wisconsin, not long after we met and he invited me to come with him.

I accepted and took him to all of my favorite haunts in Madison; we have been running together, mostly at 100 mph, ever since. What I would say about our time together is that if you are hanging out with Kid Rock and Chris Chelios, do not expect to be home before 6:00 in the morning.

So Kid Rock threw us a party in 2002 at the Jefferson Beach Grill in Saint Clair Shores, Michigan. He had his entire band there, and they played for two hours. Many fans found out about it and things got a little crazy by the end.

It's funny the things you remember; for example, I will never forget goalie Dominik Hasek getting sick while trying to smoke cigars. It was a memorable evening.

That summer, I got my chance to spend two days with the Stanley Cup. I took it to my Malibu Beach home in August and held a memorable beach party, and then in early September, before training camp started, I took it to Evergreen Park in Chicago.

Taking a Stanley Cup I had earned with the Red Wings to Chicago came with some concern. Many Blackhawks fans considered me a traitor for allowing the trade to Detroit. Remember, I had said in a television interview that I would never play for the Red Wings.

But I felt strongly about bringing the Cup home to the area where I had grown up. When I had won the Stanley Cup in 1986, it was before players were given the opportunity to spend a day with it, so this was my first chance.

Evergreen Park may have been Blackhawks country, but these were my South Side people. I had attended Southeast Elementary School and Central Junior High School in the area.

When my former 101st Street neighbors and fans started lining up at 7:30 in the morning at the Evergreen Park Village Hall, I knew I had the right decision. Plenty of people were still angry with me, but some of them were willing to hold their noses and celebrate. About 800 people came through to see the Stanley Cup. Many were wearing Blackhawks jerseys, but they came to see me. They talked to me, snapped photos, and I signed every autograph they wanted.

"I know people here still have some ill feelings that I won this with Detroit, but I'm proud to be a Chicagoan and always will be," I told the *Chicago Tribune*. "I'm also proud to share this championship with them."

AFTER WE WON IN 2002, Bowman retired. We knew things would be different under a new head coach, but we expected it to be a smooth transition because Dave Lewis, who had been our assistant coach under Bowman, was taking over.

Lewis was a nice guy, and everyone liked him. We believed it would work out.

We were wrong.

Lewis had been the good cop on our team and he had strong relationships with the players. But things are different when you are a head coach. You can't be sympathetic to all of our concerns.

Poor Dave. We ate him alive.

Ice time was always the problem, and Lewis was overwhelmed because he was trying to please too many people. No one ever dared question Bowman about who was playing how many minutes. But players were constantly in Lewis' office lobbying for playing time.

Lewis took me off the power play, but I didn't say anything about it because we had just won the Stanley Cup. Besides, at my age, I didn't care about whether I was on the power play or not.

My situation changed when Mike Babcock was hired to replace Lewis.

While I never felt like he had any animosity toward me on a personal level, the only frustration I had in my days in Detroit was my inability to convince Mike Babcock that I could do more than he believed I could.

From the first day he came to the Red Wings in 2005, he started to chip away at my opportunities. I did everything I could to earn more playing time, but he only wanted me to fill the role he had in mind for me, and offered me no chance to expand that role.

The season before Babcock arrived, I was playing 21 minutes per game; during his first season I went down to just over 18 minutes per game.

As I said, the give-and-take between player and coach over playing time is as old as the game itself. So before I go on talking about my relationship with Babcock, I should point out that his obligation was to the team, not to me. Yes, I wanted more playing time, but he obviously felt like he had better options. I never felt as if he disliked me personally. In fact, he was often quoted saying he admired the qualities I had.

I offer this look at our relationship just to give everyone an understanding of how a player reacts when he feels as if he isn't being given the opportunity to do everything he felt he was capable of.

At that time in my career, I thought I could still do more than Babcock did. It doesn't mean I'm right or he's right. That's just the nature of the player-coach relationship.

When I played in Chicago, there were stories about whether I was getting along with this coach or that coach. I would say that just because I don't agree with everything a coach does not mean that I don't respect what he is doing.

If I were an NHL coach, I would be worried if I had players on my team who *didn't* want more playing time or players who *didn't* lobby to get on the power play or to kill penalties. You want your players to crave an expanded role.

To Babcock, doling out playing time to me and the rest of the boys wasn't personal. To him, it was just business. We had several meetings but there was no changing his mind. That was difficult for me to accept because I had always played for coaches who had complete trust in my abilities.

It was such a strange situation, because sometimes I would play well and he would still be unhappy with me if I hadn't precisely followed his game plan.

Once, I used a breakout that worked well in a game. Afterward, he called me into his office and said he didn't want me to ever do it again.

"But it worked," I said.

"I don't care," he said. "If you don't want to play the way I want you to play, then you can go play for Mike Keenan again."

Deep down, I probably knew he had a point. But it was almost as if my mind wouldn't allow me to play the way Babcock wanted me to play. He wanted me to be a shot-blocker and to play less instinctually than I always had in the past. I had been a quality penalty-killer my entire career but Mike's style felt unnatural for me. Throughout my career, I had worked to get on the guys before they shot, to disrupt the shot before it happened. My philosophy was that if an opponent didn't get the shot off, he couldn't score. I went from being a good penalty-killer to a terrible penalty-killer. Plus, I broke my leg twice blocking shots.

The secret to my success was having a vision for the game, a sense for what was about to happen. The great Ted Williams once said that he didn't guess, he anticipated. That's how I played hockey. I would read and react. When Babcock asked me to change, it was like asking a quarterback to only run the play he was given without the freedom to call an audible if he senses an opponent's vulnerability at the line of scrimmage.

I understood why Babcock was asking me to do that. I was 43 when he became coach of the Red Wings, and I was 47 when I quit playing for him. At the end of my career, I wasn't a top-four defenseman. But my competitive spirit didn't know how old I was and it wanted me to play the way I always had.

Undoubtedly, Babcock grew weary of me lobbying for power play time as well. I tried to be clever about it. I asked someone to put a video clip together featuring all of my power play goals. I presented it to Mike to show him what I was capable of accomplishing.

That didn't work either, but it was worth a shot.

The only time I did feel like things got personal was when Babcock barely played me at the Winter Classic between the Red Wings and the Blackhawks at Chicago's Wrigley Field.

Both general manager Ken Holland and assistant GM Jim Nill had told me I would play in that game, considering that it was my hometown and it meant a lot to me. Everybody knew playing in that game was meaningful to me. I believe Holland and Nill must have asked Babcock to use me.

What he did was dress seven defensemen, start me, then only gave me four or five shifts in the entire game. My total ice time was under two minutes.

Obviously, I was angry and insulted. But from Babcock's perspective, I'm sure he was playing the lineup that he believed gave him the best opportunity to win.

In 2008, I played 69 games for the Red Wings in the regular season and 14 of the first 15 games in the playoffs. We had just finished knocking off the Dallas Stars, and I was standing at the mirror shaving in the dressing room when Babcock walked in and said, "You are done. You are not playing any more in the playoffs."

He decided to go with veteran Andreas Lilja. In fairness to Babcock, I wasn't playing all that well. I didn't believe I was hurting the team but I wasn't helping the team the way I wanted to either. Still, it was a tough pill to swallow. I sat without complaint and worked every day in practice to stay ready in case someone was injured. I didn't play a single game in the Final and we ended up winning the Stanley Cup. So how can I argue with Babcock's decision?

I tried to be a team player even when I wasn't in the lineup. The team song that season was The Who's "Baba O'Riley." I think I've established that I don't like any song that is overplayed.

But before Game 6 in Pittsburgh, I walked into the dressing room before the game and put that song on the stereo.

"This is the last time I'm playing this song," I said, loud enough for everyone to hear. "This ends tonight."

I put on my gear before the game even though I knew I wasn't going to play, and when the boys came in after the first period I was still sitting there in my gear. When they came into the room after the second period, I still had my gear on. This was my team and I wanted to feel like a part of it.

As my teammates were competing on the ice, I couldn't stand to watch on the television. It was too stressful. Jim Paek, one of our AHL assistant coaches in Grand Rapids, was in there with me. He sat in a shower stall. He also had trouble watching.

But when we won I celebrated as if I had scored the series-winning goal. I felt as if I had contributed. At 46, I became the oldest player ever to be a member of a Stanley Cup–winning team.

This section about my struggles to earn playing time under Babcock is not to imply he was wrong in how he handled me. Like I said, how can I argue that Babcock doesn't properly use his personnel? Look at his record. The NHL is a bottom-line business. It's about winning, and Babcock has gotten results.

After the clinching game, Holland told me on the ice that he was appreciative of how I handled the playing time issue. He told the *Detroit News* that he believed I still had "lots of hockey" left in me.

LATER IN THE OFF-SEASON, Holland gave me another contract that would pay me $750,000 for the 2008–09 season. He told me that if we won another Stanley Cup, he would give me another one-year contract for the 2009–10 season.

Holland always talks about how I rode my bicycle 20 miles from my home in Bloomfield Hills, Michigan, to Joe Louis Arena to sign the contract that would take me beyond my 47th birthday.

But that wasn't unusual for me, especially during the summer months in Michigan. It was a normal occurrence for me to ride from my home to my restaurant in Dearborn, and then from there to my restaurant near Comerica Park.

By the time I returned home I would have logged 60 miles on my bike. If I just went from my house to Cheli's Chili Bar near the ballpark, it was 38 miles round trip. It was essentially an hour each way. People who lived downtown would yell, "Hey, Hockey Man!" as I pedaled past them on Woodward Avenue.

I used to do it both in daylight and at night, but riding at night seemed too dangerous after someone tried to run me off the road, seemingly on purpose. At that point, I decided to ride only in daylight hours.

The 2008–09 season didn't go as well for me as it did for our team. I broke my leg in the preseason, and as a result I only played 28 games. By that point, I had given up trying to convince Mike

I was fortunate enough to play for the Montreal Canadiens, one of the greatest franchises in hockey. To be honest, I probably wasn't ready for the responsibility that came with being an American captain of a Canadian team in a bilingual city.
(Getty Images)

Here I am tussling with the Flyers' Brian Propp in front of the net. It was not the first or last run-in I had with Propp. (Getty Images)

Being traded to my hometown and playing for the Blackhawks was a dream come true. My biggest regret about those nine seasons in Chicago is that we never brought home a Stanley Cup. The closest we came was in 1992, when we were swept in the Final by Mario Lemieux and the Penguins (below). (AP Images/Getty Images)

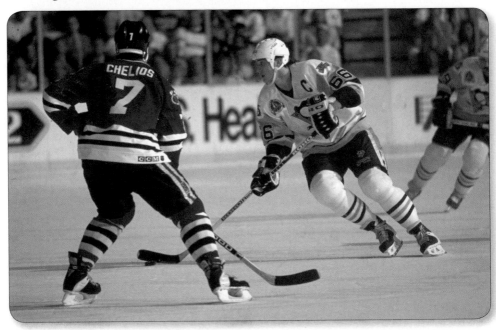

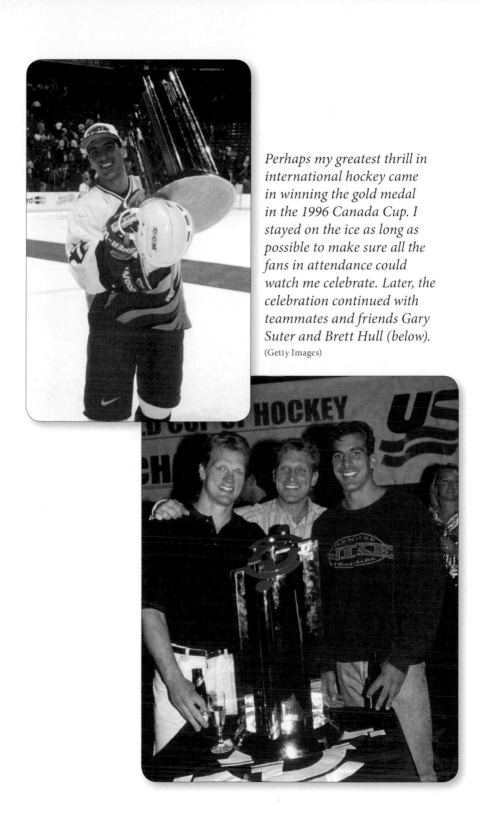

Perhaps my greatest thrill in international hockey came in winning the gold medal in the 1996 Canada Cup. I stayed on the ice as long as possible to make sure all the fans in attendance could watch me celebrate. Later, the celebration continued with teammates and friends Gary Suter and Brett Hull (below).
(Getty Images)

The rivalry between the Blackhawks and Red Wings was so heated that fans at Joe Louis Arena once hung my jersey in effigy. I also famously said I would "never" play for Detroit. (Newscom)

After the Blackhawks made it clear I wasn't in their future plans, I decided to let bygones be bygones and become a Red Wing, partly to stay close to my family in Chicago. Joining a team led by a guy like Steve Yzerman allowed me to focus on hockey and not locker room politics. (Dave Reginek)

By the time I won my first Stanley Cup with the Red Wings in 2002, the fans had accepted me as one of their own. (AP Images)

I'll never forget having my family with me on the ice after defeating Carolina in Game 5: (clockwise) my wife, Tracee, and our kids Caley, Dean, Tara, and Jake).
(Getty Images)

In 2008, I was part of another championship team in Detroit. After a parade through the city, I was again able to celebrate with my family, and this time we were joined by my parents. (Dave Reginek)

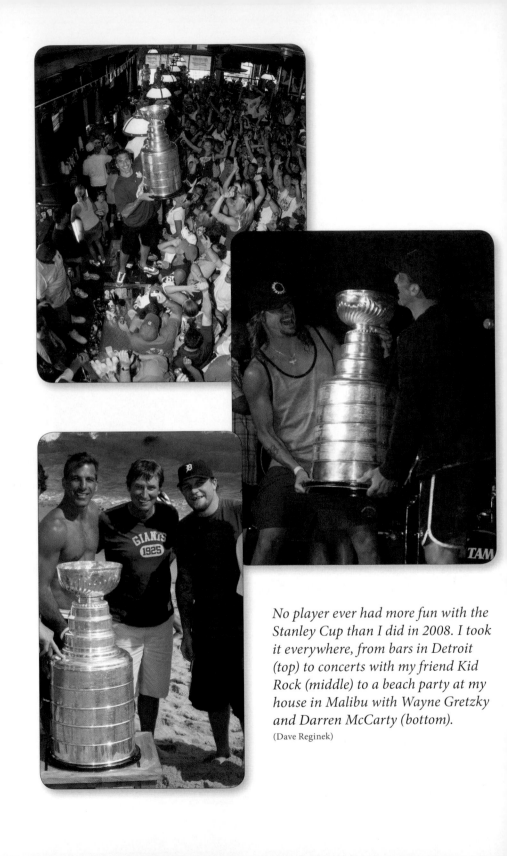

No player ever had more fun with the Stanley Cup than I did in 2008. I took it everywhere, from bars in Detroit (top) to concerts with my friend Kid Rock (middle) to a beach party at my house in Malibu with Wayne Gretzky and Darren McCarty (bottom).

(Dave Reginek)

Even though my ice time in the game was limited, playing in the 2009 Winter Classic at Wrigley Field is something I'll never forget.
(Getty Images)

After I left Detroit I joined the Chicago Wolves of the AHL. The fans treated me great; it was the first time I felt like people in Chicago were ready to welcome me back home.
(USA Today Sports Images)

Despite some boos from the fans who still can't forgive and forget, I appreciated the Blackhawks honoring me at the United Center in 2010. No matter what some people might think, I will always be a Chicagoan in my heart. (Getty Images)

My Hall of Fame induction was a great chance for me to get together with my friends in the Malibu Mob, including (top) Jeff Sweet, John C. McGinley, D.B. Sweeney, Nate Heydari (bottom), Don Wildman, Tony Danza, John McEnroe, and John Cusack. (Dave Reginek)

Because they have such busy schedules, it meant a lot to me that friends like Michael Jordan and Tie Domi made time to help me celebrate such a special occasion. (Dave Reginek)

Being inducted into the Hockey Hall of Fame was the culmination of an incredible and improbable ride, one that began on the beaches in San Diego and ended up in Toronto. (Dave Reginek)

that I deserved more playing time. I even made myself a healthy scratch on one occasion.

My son Jake was playing youth hockey for the Little Caesars team. Late in the Red Wings' season, Jake's team was competing for the national championship in Pittsburgh, and I wanted to be there.

The problem was that Mike wanted to rest some of his regulars, and I was scheduled to play so that Brian Rafalski could sit. Without telling Mike, I went to Rafalski and asked him to play for me.

When I told him I wanted to see my son play, he was completely on board with my plan.

I hadn't cleared that with Mike, though, and he was stunned to see Rafalski dressing for the game.

"What are you doing here?" he asked.

"Chelios asked me to play for him," Rafalski said.

My son won the national championship, his third in four years, and I was back in time for practice the next day. As was always the case, Babcock and I were the first ones at the rink.

I was shaving in the sauna when he confronted me.

"This is my team, not your team," he told me sternly. "I make lineup decisions, not you."

"Okay," I said.

What could I say? He certainly had a right to be mad. If he was looking for an argument, he wasn't going to get one from me. I certainly would not have done that earlier in the season, but by then it was well established that I was not in Mike's plans. I think my teammates all understood why I did what I did. At the end of the day, nothing is more important to me than my family.

I played six games in the playoffs, including the clinching Game 5 against the Chicago Blackhawks in the Western Conference Final.

Nicklas Lidstrom's injury gave me the opportunity to play in that game and I almost scored in overtime. On the next shift, center Darren Helm scored at 3:58 to give us a 2–1 win that put us in the Stanley Cup Final.

I didn't know it at the time, but that was my last shift in a Red Wings jersey. That it was a quality shift is important to me. When I played, I didn't like to leave anything in the tank.

The 2009 Stanley Cup Final was a rematch of the 2008 Stanley Cup Final, only this time the Penguins ended up winning a Game 7 in Detroit. With Lidstrom healthy again, there was no room for me in the lineup.

After talking to Holland that summer, I reached the conclusion that it was time to end my Red Wings career. Holland had always treated me with great respect, but I felt as if now I was standing in the way of younger players whose time had come. We had lost defenseman Kyle Quincey on waivers to the Los Angeles Kings at the start of the 2008–09 season because we had too many defensemen. I didn't want the organization to lose people out of its loyalty to me. I didn't like the idea of being a third-pairing defenseman that was blocking the path for a skilled young player. That is not who I am.

I told Holland that I was ready to move on, even though I wasn't 100 percent certain that I wanted to retire. I figured that if someone called and offered me a spot, I would consider playing another season.

But my phone didn't ring over a long, hot summer.

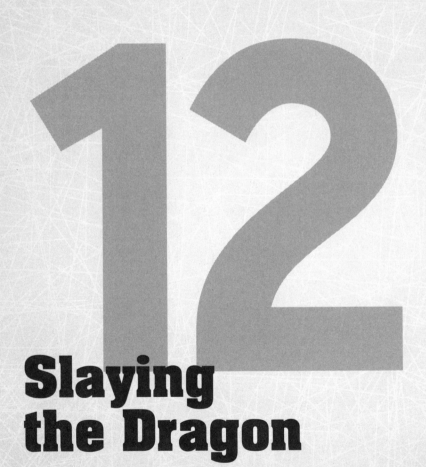

12
Slaying
the Dragon

M y dad probably remembers August 31, 1996, as the day he gave his daughter's hand away in marriage— and angrily shook his fist at his son.

As soon as my sister Eleni said "I do" and kissed her new husband Donald, I bolted out the Chicago church door to catch a flight to Philadelphia for the opening game of the World Cup.

I couldn't bring myself to tell my dad that I was leaving the wedding early, so he was furious when he realized that I was putting hockey ahead of family.

My father believed a family member doesn't bail on a Greek wedding, but I believed I couldn't bail on a group of guys who were also like family to me.

That was the day of the opening game against Canada, and my American buddies had been calling me for two weeks telling me they needed me to help slay the dragon. Sometimes they would call 2:00 in the morning.

I had been trying to beat Canada for a long time, and with the arrival of players such as Bill Guerin, Keith Tkachuk, and Derian Hatcher, among others, it looked as if we finally had the physical presence necessary to get that job done.

It wasn't as if we were going to surprise anyone. A month before the tournament, the media was talking about the possibility that the Americans might finally have their day.

My buddy Jeremy Roenick fanned the flames and fired up our competition by saying publicly that we were going to win the tournament.

As it turned out, Roenick ended up in a contract battle and didn't play because he couldn't risk getting hurt.

My timing on leaving the wedding had to be perfect in order to make the game in Philadelphia. My limousine had a police escort from the airport to the arena. Although I missed the pregame skate, I was dressed and ready for the opening faceoff.

Pool play or not, this game was important, because we needed to show the Canadians that this World Cup was going to be different than the 1991 Canada Cup, where we advanced to the final only to be beaten in two straight games by the Canadians. In that tournament, we lost three times to them, counting the loss in the preliminary round.

Before the 1996 game was a minute old, Tkachuk broke Claude Lemieux's nose in a fight. Not long after, Hatcher decked Canada's Eric Lindros behind the net.

We won 5–3, and I believe the Canadians understood right then that the American team now had some teeth. The 1996 U.S. team was more skilled and much tougher than previous U.S. squads.

During the postgame revelry in the dressing room, I told the media the story of walking out of my sister's wedding before the reception. I explained to reporters how my mother had to hold back my father as I left the church. I figured my sister and her husband would understand, but I knew it was going to take a while for my father to get over it.

Reporters listened intently to the tale and one of them, thinking about the good story it would make, said, "This is great."

"Great for you, maybe," I said. "But you don't have to face my dad."

BEATING CANADA WAS ALWAYS important to me because I both hated and admired their arrogance when it comes to hockey.

Canadians say hockey is their game, but the truth is that hockey is the Canadians' *only* game. The vast majority of their best athletes play hockey, while America's top athletes play a variety of sports.

The Canadians' arrogance, however, is also what keeps them strong in international hockey. They come into every tournament expecting to win.

In the preliminary round of the 1996 World Cup, we defeated Russia, Canada, and Slovakia to win our pool and earn a bye into the semifinals.

We faced Russia in a game that was played in Ottawa. We were stunned that the Canadian fans rooted loudly for the Russians throughout the game.

Our coach Ron Wilson said after the game that it felt like the game was being played in Moscow.

Canadian fans were also hard on my buddy Brett Hull, a Canadian-born player who had been part of the U.S. program since the 1980s (his mother was American). Canadian fans didn't much care that Hull had been on Team USA before; now that he had established himself as an NHL goal-scoring star, they chanted "Traitor. Traitor. Traitor."

Hull scored a couple of goals to help us defeat the Russians 5–2 much to the dismay of the Canadians in attendance.

The fact that those fans were rooting for the Russians was yet another indication that Canadians understood how talented our group was. It seemed as if we had our hosts worried.

The Canadians' anti-American stance in Ottawa probably helped my relationship with my father. Watching the tournament on television, he was incensed about how the fans had rooted for Russia against us. Suddenly I was the sympathetic figure. He was madder at the Canadians than he was at me.

Canada needed a double-overtime win against Sweden to earn the right to play us in the best-of-three World Cup final.

Unlike the fans in Ottawa, we were rooting for Canada to win that game; if we won the World Cup without beating Canada, we would have never heard the end of it. Not only did we want to win, we wanted to humble the reigning champions.

Canadians became smug again after my future Red Wings teammate Steve Yzerman scored in overtime to beat us in Game 1 in Philadelphia.

We were all sure that the linesman had missed an offside call before the goal was scored.

No one on the Canadian team offered any bulletin board material after the victory, but you know they were thinking that nothing had changed for the American program.

However, our confidence level was still high. We expected to play better in Game 2, and we certainly did, winning 5–2. Hullie scored another goal.

One of Adam Foote's shots hit me, and the puck deflected directly to Hull, who scored on a breakaway.

I went hard after Lindros and we ended up slashing and hacking each other the entire game. The next day, the Montreal newspapers suggested Game 3 would be Canada's most important game since the 1972 Summit Series, when the Canadians had defeated the Soviets.

Mark Messier had missed Game 2 with the "flu", but he said he would be ready for the deciding game, as if there was any doubt.

Coach Ron Wilson talked about beating the lion in the lion's den. We were expecting the game to be a war and it was. After Tkachuk received a game misconduct for slashing Foote, Foote scored to give Canada a 2–1 lead with 7:10 left.

Less than four minutes later, Hull redirected Hatcher's shot into the net to tie the game.

Then my Chicago Blackhawks teammate Tony Amonte scored perhaps the biggest goal of his career to give us a 3–2 lead. Hatcher then scored on a 180-foot empty-netter and Adam Deadmarsh added another as Team USA had its best international win since the Miracle on Ice 16 years earlier.

Hull had never won anything in his life and he didn't even know how to celebrate. He asked me what to do.

"Just throw your shit up in the air," I said.

Two things I want to point out about that triumph in Montreal. First, I stayed on the ice for a long time after the game because I wanted the Canadians to see me celebrating.

Second, I bring up that World Cup championship every chance I get when talking to Canadians because it irritates them to this day.

THE CANADIANS DIDN'T GET their revenge until six years later at the 2002 Olympics. Although we lost to them in the gold medal game, I have always maintained that the games in that tournament were without a doubt the best hockey games I ever played in my life.

I also loved playing for coach Herb Brooks.

What's forgotten now is that I was far from a lock to make that U.S. team in 2002. I was 40 years old, and the 1998 squad had not performed well in Japan. Herb was contemplating changes to the U.S. roster, and I had only played 24 games the previous season in Detroit after a major knee injury.

So he had plenty of reasons not to include me, but he said he wanted to sit down with me before he decided. He flew out to Los Angeles and we talked about what had happened in Nagano. I could see him soaking in everything I was telling him. He told people that my analysis of 1998 is what convinced him of my value to the team.

It probably wasn't what I said to Brooks as much as how I said it. I'm sure he knew from talking to me that I care deeply about Team USA winning in international hockey.

I don't recall all of the topics we talked about, but I remember telling him that I felt our group played best when we had specific instructions on what we were trying to accomplish. Ron Wilson may have respected us too much as players. Because all of us were NHL stars, he asked us for our opinions on how we should break out and attack. I think we were better when we were just told what to do. In 1998, we had too many opinions and ended up with a system that was too simple. It diluted the value of our team's overall skill level.

Brooks told me that I was on the team, and by the time he flew home to Minnesota I was named captain.

It was clear immediately that Brooks coached the way I like to be coached. He was tough and smart, and he knew how and when to make adjustments to help his team be successful. He knew when to rein in players and when to just let them play.

Now, that wasn't exactly my initial impression of him. I loved Badger Bob Johnson, my coach at Wisconsin, and he and Brooks did not get along. Being a team guy, I was on Johnson's side in their feud, so I disliked Brooks on general principle.

But over the years I talked to many of his former players and always heard the same thing: yes, Brooks was tough on the 1980 team, but when it was all over none of the players had a bad word to say about him.

That was good enough for me; anyone associated with that Miracle on Ice team is gold to me. Those guys are the untouchables. They can do no wrong.

The 2002 Olympic tournament could not have started better: we downed Finland 6–0, thumped Belarus 8–1, and in between played a hard-fought 2–2 tie with Russia. With Igor Larionov, Pavel Bure, Sergei Fedorov, Ilya Kovalchuk, and others on that squad, the Russians probably had the best offensive talent in the tournament.

The television ratings of that game were the highest for any hockey game since Brooks and the Americans beat the Soviets in 1980 at Lake Placid.

We beat Germany 5–0 in the quarterfinals, meaning at that point we had outscored our opponents 21–3.

Meanwhile, the Russians had beaten the Czechs 1–0 to set up a rematch with us in the semifinals.

Mike Modano played brilliantly in that tournament and Tkachuk was a beast. Goalie Mike Richter was on top of his game. We were a confident group, but we knew the Russians would test us. The game was played on February 22—the 22nd anniversary of the Miracle on Ice.

At a practice before that game, Herb Brooks passed out USA Hockey pens to everyone and told us, "Write your own story."

Those pens were Brooks' way of saying this tournament wasn't about him or the 1980 team. This tournament was about us, the current group, and the history we wanted to make ourselves.

All the reporters covering the tournament wanted to write about Brooks' triumphant return, but he kept telling everyone that it was my team, not his. He said the Chelios "stamp" was on it. But Brooks was still pulling all of the levers, and he had a handle on how everyone was feeling and playing.

Most of the Americans who played in our 3–2 semifinal win against Russia will say it was the best game they have ever played. It was up-and-down, thrill-per-minute hockey.

We built a 3–0 lead after two periods on goals by Bill Guerin, Scott Young, and Phil Housley, and then hung on for dear life. Richter played out of this world. The Russians could have easily won both games we played. Both games were pressure-filled battles. It felt as if we had emptied our tanks to beat the Russians in that second meeting.

After that game, Brooks' record in the Olympics was 10–0–2.

WE COULD CERTAINLY FEEL the pressure heading into that gold medal game against Canada. This was the most important meeting between the two countries since the 1996 World Cup.

I remember sitting next to my buddy Gary Suter before the game and hearing him mumble, "Wow, this is a really big game."

Suter's nervousness was painfully obvious.

"It's no problem, Sutes," I told him. "We've either won a gold medal or a silver, so just go out there and relax."

Even as the words came out of my mouth I knew they would have no impact on Suter. He was always a worrier.

Of course, I didn't make the situation any better by saying things like, "I don't want to be too close to you when we walk off the bus." Suter was still concerned about some crazed Canadian fan looking for retribution for his hit on Gretzky years ago.

When the game started, Suter was still trying to calm himself down. We won the faceoff, the puck went to Suter, and he fired it into our bench.

A moment later, another faceoff, Suter had the puck, and again drove it out of play.

Back when Darryl Sutter was the head coach in Chicago, he'd sometimes yell at Suter while Gary was on the ice. Sutter thought he was helping, but it would throw Suter off his game and ended up doing more harm than good.

Seeing Suter pressing, Brett Hull, sitting on the bench, stood up and yelled, "He's been Darryl-ized!"

That made everyone laugh and probably calmed everyone down, including Suter.

Even though we lost to Canada 5–2, I felt we could have won that game. We had a 1–0 lead after a goal by Tony Amonte, and Roenick tried a toe-drag move on a 3-on-1 break but we didn't get a shot on goal.

What really hurt was an injury suffered by Tkachuk in the semifinals against Russia. He was on fire in that tournament, and we could have used his physical presence against Canada.

Give the Canadians credit; they just kept coming at us and refused to back down. Their defensemen kept pressing. Joe Sakic played well in that game.

After Paul Kariya and Jarome Iginla scored to give Canada a 2–1 lead, Brian Rafalski scored to tie the game. Then Sakic scored to give Canada the lead again. We were still scrapping to tie until Iginla redirected Yzerman's shot with four minutes remaining to give Canada a two-goal lead.

In hindsight, we started to wear out in the gold medal game. The semifinal win against Russia had been emotionally draining. While we were fighting for our tournament lives, Canada had a much easier game against Belarus, who had shocked Sweden to advance but were out of miracles.

Brooks had decided not to name Derian Hatcher to the team because he didn't think he skated well enough for the wider Salt Lake City ice surface.

Maybe we could have used him against Canada, but we'll never know. In short international tournaments, it's difficult to know why teams win or lose. Sometimes teams get on a roll, and sometimes they don't.

If you look at the 2004 World Cup, we lost to Finland 2–1 in the semifinal game. When you compare the two rosters, you would think we would have won that game nine times out of 10. But we didn't get it done that day.

In 2002, on the day of the gold medal game, Canada was the better team. It's that simple.

Despite the loss, the game against Canada was a great game to play. We won an Olympic silver medal. I try to remember that. And playing for Brooks was an unreal experience. I could see why guys would go through a wall for him.

International competition never got old to me. I played in four Olympics and wore the USA jersey 10 times in my career. I hated losing to Canada. In fact, I hated losing, period, when I wore a Team USA jersey. When I played for the Americans at the 1984 Olympics, I was so disappointed with our performance that I traded my Team USA jacket to sportswriter Ed Swift for a *Sports Illustrated* jacket.

When it was announced that I had been elected to the Hockey Hall of Fame, members of the media asked me several times which jersey I would be wearing in my photo.

Fortunately, the Hockey Hall of Fame doesn't follow the same protocol embraced by the Baseball Hall of Fame, which apparently does require that inductees pick a team.

That would have been difficult for me because I am the only player to play 400 or more games with three different teams.

In a Hall of Fame program, I'm featured in a Blackhawks jersey because I played the most games for that team.

But if I was forced to pick a jersey, I might go with a Team USA sweater…just to piss off the Canadians.

13
State of
the Union

W hen Bob Goodenow was fired as executive director of the NHL Players Association in the wee hours of a July morning in 2005, I was trying to prevent it from happening.

I had called then–Colorado Avalanche defenseman Rob Blake and asked him to help me get on the conference call when the NHLPA executive committee voted to fire Goodenow. I was an assistant player representative and I believed I had the right to be part of the discussion.

But the word we received from the chain of command was that this conference call was restricted to NHLPA executive committee officers only.

I didn't believe then that a secretive meeting was the way to handle the situation, and I still don't today. My opinion was that when you belong to a union, you have the right to be involved in all union meetings, including one where the fate of the union leader is being determined.

The fact that this meeting was held basically in the middle of the night simply underlined the fact that this was the wrong way for our union to be conducting business.

Trevor Linden was the president of the NHLPA then. He was a hard-nosed player and respected by his teammates. But

I think he received bad advice, or was misguided, in the way he handled the Goodenow firing.

He has always said that Ted Saskin was hired after Goodenow was fired, but I believe it happened the other way around.

Los Angeles Kings forward Trent Klatt and Carolina Hurricanes goalie Arturs Irbe were committee members who tried to do the right thing. They knew Goodenow should not be fired in this manner, but they were ignored because Linden had the four votes he needed to fire Bob.

It was clear to me that the constitution had not been followed. My beliefs were supported by the findings of a 66-page report issued by famed lawyer Sheila Block, who was hired to do an independent review of what had transpired. One of Block's findings was that Saskin and the executive committee had ignored the union's constitution in the handling of Goodenow's dismissal and Saskin's hiring.

Maybe it was time for Goodenow to step down, but firing him the way it was done was not a professional way to handle that situation. Goodenow's mother had died, and it was a difficult time for him. He had served the NHLPA well. While he was the NHLPA executive director, salaries had risen dramatically. The NHLPA was considered a strong union for many years. If he was going to be asked to leave, it should have been handled respectfully. We owed him a graceful exit.

However, Goodenow was also at fault for allowing this to happen. He knew this was not the way it should have been handled. I had warned him what was happening but he chose to let it slide.

We had lost the entire 2004–05 season because of the lockout. Before the owners took that drastic step, Bob should have called together a group of 30 or 40 veteran players to hear our point of view.

Bob was adamant about opposing the salary cap, but many veterans believed it was an inevitability. Many of us were willing to concede that point in order to save the season. That's what happened during the 1994–95 lockout; veteran players talked with Bob and we ended up finding a way to salvage a 48-game season.

One of the problems with the NHLPA, and it's a problem with all unions, is that it's difficult to convince members to become engaged in the process.

When I raised questions about the process that led to Saskin replacing Goodenow, I was dismissed as a lone voice in the woods.

It was my belief that Linden was in over his head and was listening to the wrong people. I remember watching him try to make a point to players at a meeting in Vancouver and seeing Saskin nudging him under the table, as if to tell Linden he wasn't helping his cause.

When Saskin's deal to become executive director was announced, he said 86 percent of the players had approved it. But the Block report concluded that only 55 percent of the players had initially approved it.

Given that the players had millions of dollars at stake, it was ridiculous that we rushed into the Saskin decision the way we did. I'm clearly not the only player who realized this fact. There were others who knew the executive board had acted inappropriately. That's why it took three votes to formally hire Saskin. It wasn't about legality or who had power—it was about doing the right thing. Irbe and Klatt also didn't think it was appropriate that the leadership group had talked to Saskin before making a decision on Bob.

The NHLPA had more than 700 members, but it wasn't easy getting the word out about what was happening. But over time I convinced others that our union had been hijacked by a select few.

My former Blackhawks teammate Steve Larmer had resigned from the NHLPA board in 2005 because he believed Saskin wasn't following the NHLPA constitution. His resignation brought more focus to the idea that Saskin's hiring needed to be reviewed.

Our voices were finally heard. But it wasn't until May 10, 2007, that the player representatives voted unanimously to fire Ted. The final vote was 22–0 because some player reps were playing at the World Championships and Edmonton's Shawn Horcoff was the best man at a wedding.

When his dismissal was approved, Saskin had already been on paid leave because he was accused of reading players' private emails.

(Later, Block's independent report on what had transpired in Goodenow's removal concluded that we needed more checks and balances in our constitution. She also discovered that Goodenow and Saskin had both taped conversations with people, including players, without notifying them. While it wasn't illegal, it sure seemed shady.)

WHEN SASKIN WAS REMOVED, I believed the NHLPA was headed in the right direction. After all, the decision to fire Saskin had been unanimous. Previously, he had supporters among the player representatives. But when everyone looked at the evidence presented, it was clear that he had to go.

He was succeeded by Paul Kelly, the former Boston prosecutor who had helped topple Alan Eagleson, the former NHLPA executive director. He didn't last two years before he was fired in another late-night voting session.

In my opinion, the Kelly firing was handled just as inappropriately as the Goodenow firing.

I was on the selection committee that hired Kelly and I believed that he was the right man for the job. Our group was very interested in Donald Fehr, who was retiring as executive director of the Major League Baseball Players Association. But Fehr wasn't interested in the position at the time. We also liked Fehr's assistant, Michael Weiner, but he wasn't interested either because he was planning to succeed Fehr at the MLBPA.

It came down to Kelly and another qualified candidate (whose identity I am protecting because that was his wish). We went with Kelly. If there had not been a witch hunt to bring him down, I think Kelly would have done a good job for us.

Kelly's misdeed, which caused his termination, was reviewing notes from a Las Vegas player representative meeting after he had been asked to leave the room. His argument was that he looked at the notes to make sure the constitution wasn't being violated. But he was clearly wrong for looking at them without the permission of the player representatives.

The saddest aspect of Kelly's dismissal is that we probably would have given him permission to look at the notes if he had asked us.

While he was out of the room, NHLPA general counsel Ian Penny was given a contract extension. Penny had talked to Kelly about an extension, but Kelly had asked him to wait until he took care of some other issues first. The players gave Penny the extension while Kelly was out of the room. According to our constitution, the executive director is only supposed to be asked to leave the room if the player representatives are talking about him specifically. Talking about Penny while Kelly wasn't in the room should not have been allowed, according to my opinion of how we should have conducted our business.

The Penny contract extension had not been an agenda item. That was another issue I had about the way NHLPA did business. It always bothered me when we would show up at meetings and suddenly find ourselves making major decisions without having advance notice the issue was even going to be discussed.

My objection to Kelly's firing was again about how the voting was conducted. We did it at 3:00 AM on August 31, 2009, in a Chicago hotel. Nothing totally on the up-and-up happens at meetings conducted at 3:00 in the morning. Again, most of us didn't know the Kelly vote was coming.

I abstained on the vote because I wanted to go back and discuss it with my teammates. Nobody else felt that way.

Whether Kelly would have been a quality NHLPA executive director, we will never know. But the committee that hired him believed he would have been the right guy to negotiate the last collective bargaining agreement.

What we liked was that he knew the game in addition to having a legal background. Kelly had been around the game for a long time. He had a strong reputation as a player advocate, and he had a sterling reputation as a lawyer. I believed he was a stand-up guy.

After the Kelly firing, my Detroit teammate Nicklas Lidstrom, along with Boston Bruin Mark Recchi, Blake, and I were named as a review committee to look at what happened.

Penny was named interim director, and he and I ended up having issues.

I felt bad about that, because I respected Ian for what he had done for the NHLPA. He had helped us remove Saskin. A lot of players liked Ian. Up until that point, I always felt he put the best interest of the players first.

Our issues centered on what I considered Ian's impatience. In his mind, the NHLPA was falling apart and he wanted to change things immediately. I wanted the players to have a say in everything that was done. We may have agreed on the overall objectives, but if we made changes without players having a voice, weren't we just repeating the mistakes of the past?

Penny resigned two months after Kelly was fired, saying he felt that "he could no longer work in the present environment."

There's no question he wanted me off the review committee, mostly because I didn't want major decisions being made until a new executive director could be hired.

In addition to Penny's departure, Larmer had resigned from his NHLPA advisory post and blasted me publicly as he walked out the door. Outside counsel Paul Cavalluzzo also resigned, as did advisory board members Dan O'Neill and Ron Lloyd.

Larmer said it would be disastrous for the NHLPA if I wasn't removed from my position on the review committee.

That was difficult for me to hear because Larmer is one of the most honest guys I've ever met. Penny and I were among those who talked him into coming back and working again for NHLPA after he resigned the first time.

But I understood Larmer's position. He was Penny's friend. He believed in Penny. Larmer liked it when I was the whistle-blower who was trying to remove Saskin. But he didn't like me as a whistle-blower if I was saying I didn't want Penny to be making significant moves as an interim director. Everyone likes the watch dog until he bites someone you like.

Since then, I've talked to Larmer and we have hashed out our differences. It's all water under the bridge now. He understands where I was coming from, and I certainly fully appreciate his position.

What I can tell you is that friendships were damaged as we tried to rebuild our union. But my only objective was to make sure that everything was handled professionally and properly.

We were very fortunate that we ended up with Donald Fehr in charge after the mess we had created. We tried three or four times to persuade him to get involved when we did our initial search.

The union issues cost many of us time and friendships. The lockout certainly cost me my friendship with Brendan Shanahan.

Shanahan and I are cordial when we see each other. But we don't embrace each other like old war buddies. It feels as if we were on different sides in that conflict, or at least had different agendas.

It's been almost a decade since Goodenow was toppled, but Shanahan and I never fully repaired our relationship.

Shanahan, now president of the Toronto Maple Leafs, has said to me that we should talk.

"Okay, when?" I ask.

I say that because I know he's just giving me one of those California-style "We should go out for dinner sometime" invitations. It is a polite way to bring closure to a conversation, not an actual invite.

I'm sure Shanahan doesn't care what I think about what he did during the lockout. He has his opinion, and I have mine. Probably no amount of debate would change how we feel about what happened in 2005.

As a player, I always had respect for Shanahan. He was a great teammate and player. You could count on Shanny being there for you when the game turned rough.

But I didn't like how he used his influence during the final stage of the lockout. Shanahan helped turn the tide against Goodenow, and I know that is true because he called me to try and lobby me to his side.

At one Red Wings player meeting, he told us that if we chose not to vote, Saskin had the right to view the Red Wings' vote as a "no" vote.

I said I didn't believe that should be, or would be, allowed under our constitution.

Shanahan then backed off and said that's what Saskin had told him.

I think of Shanahan every time I see one of those television commercials about the guy who gets smarter because he stayed at a Holiday Inn Express the night before.

In my opinion, Shanahan has a gift for making people believe he knows more than he really does. He was always concerned about his image. Sometimes it seemed as if he put his own best interests ahead of his teammates.

That's how I felt during the lockout. In my opinion, Shanahan did what was best for him, not what was best for his fellow NHLPA members.

Everyone knew that Shanahan had been talking to league officials during the lockout. When the smoke cleared from the work stoppage, there was a job at the NHL office waiting for Shanahan when he retired. I was not the only player who didn't like how that looked and smelled.

I don't enjoy saying this about Shanahan; I don't like going after teammates. We won a Stanley Cup together. We should be friends forever. But this issue is important, and I tell this story with the hope that a future generation of NHLPA members can avoid these difficult situations.

Plus, maybe now Shanahan will call me and we can settle our differences on this issue. I'll be waiting by the phone.

TO BE HONEST, IT was out of character for me to be involved in NHLPA politics. The two aspects of life that I don't have much use for are organized religion and politics. I don't vote. I don't like either major political party. I don't have any trust in the people involved in either religion or politics. I don't even allow those subjects to be discussed in my house.

When I first thought about writing this book, I considered including a chapter entitled "My Opinions and Thoughts on Politics and Religion." Then I just wanted to have 10 blank pages. That probably would have made it clear how much disdain I have for politics and religion.

But I became involved in the NHLPA because I believed it was important. Playing in Detroit, I got to know Ted Lindsay, who helped found the NHLPA. He paid a price for his involvement. It hurt his career. Because of his union activity, many considered Lindsay to be a troublemaker.

I felt like I owed it to Ted to continue what he started. I was in the final stages of my career when all of this was happening. I had nothing to gain by being involved. I wasn't looking for a job with the NHLPA. That's not who I am. I felt we owed it to future players to do the best we could to make sure everything was handled properly.

I see issues as black or white. I don't see gray. Either you do it right, or you don't do it. And as a hockey player, I believe you have to stand up for your teammates. That's what I believed I was doing during this NHLPA battle.

I was also thinking of the late NHL defenseman Carl Brewer, who was instrumental in bringing Alan Eagleson to justice for criminal acts Eagleson committed while with the NHLPA.

I felt as if I owed Brewer my best effort to make sure the NHLPA represented all of our members. Brewer's work is devalued if other players don't do whatever they can to make sure that union business is conducted by the book.

I wanted players to be involved in all decisions, and I wanted all procedures to be followed according our constitution. When our emails were being read, executives were being fired in the middle of the night, and four players were making all of the decisions, I believed it was time to do what I could to protect my fellow union members.

I had battled Linden in front of the net because it was my job. Maybe it was also my job to hold him accountable for what he was doing as president of the NHLPA.

14

Guilty Until
Proven Innocent

The rumor that I was planning to skewer NHL commissioner Gary Bettman during my 2013 Hall of Fame induction speech was either a fabrication or misplaced speculation.

That was neither the time nor the place for me to take a shot at Bettman. I never even considered mentioning him.

Besides, whatever I could say about Bettman would simply be piling on. He is booed in every NHL arena he enters. It doesn't seem as if fans need my help to formulate an opinion of the man. I believe players and fans understand all they need to know about Bettman.

My issue with Bettman was always about his portrayal of what his mission is as NHL commissioner.

He represents the owners' interests. He is a businessman. That is his job, and I'm sure owners are quite pleased with the work he has done for them. My beef is that he is not open about his priorities. He plays with semantics, continually spinning his words, to make it seem as if he's representing the concerns of the players and the fans.

In reality, he only represents the concerns of the owners.

I'm not saying that's wrong, because he is performing the duties that his employers are asking him to do. But at least be open about it.

I assume the main reason people thought I might slam him during my speech was because everyone in hockey knows that we have had a rocky relationship for almost two decades.

Just after Bettman and the NHL owners locked us out before the 1994–95 season, I allowed my emotions to boil over and made some statements that I soon regretted.

With television cameras rolling and tape recorders on, I said, "If I was Gary Bettman, I'd worry about my family, about my well-being right now. Some crazed fan or even a player—who knows?—might take it into his own hands and figure if they can get him out of the way, this might be settled. You hate to see something like that happen, but he took the job."

Never did I intend for my quotes to be taken as a threat. I certainly wasn't suggesting that someone should target Bettman. The meaning of those words was literal. I was saying that the situation was so emotional for fans and players that I was fearful that something awful might happen. I was not advocating for that to occur; I was worried that it might.

Those comments were made right after I had come off the ice from the last Blackhawks practice before the lockout. Coach Darryl Sutter, being the kind-hearted guy that he is, had opted to put us through a kiss-my-ass kind of practice. He made us skate until we were ready to drop. He may have been an ex-player, but Sutter didn't act like it on that day. So I was probably not in the right frame of mind when I stepped in front of the media.

But I wasn't the only angry player. Wayne Gretzky, Joe Sakic, and Cam Neely were among the prominent figures who criticized Bettman's lockout plan, although their words were more carefully chosen than mine.

When I get fired up, I move dirt with a bulldozer, not a shovel.

Because athletes make big salaries, it's assumed that we are less bothered by labor issues. But nothing could be further from the truth. If someone says you are not allowed to work, or that your working conditions are going to change, you get angry. On that day, I snapped. Reporters caught me at a time when my emotions were raw. I was still sweating from Sutter's torture session when I gave that interview. Had I been interviewed two or three hours later, after I had come to grips with the lockout, I would not have said what I said.

When the lockout was over, Bettman wanted to suspend me for those comments. But NHLPA executive director Bob Goodenow told Bettman that wasn't going to happen.

Our position was that I was locked out, and therefore no longer an NHL employee, so I was free to say whatever I wanted to say.

Chicago general manager Bob Pulford and I went to New York to discuss the situation with Bettman. We met for 45 minutes. The compromise we agreed to was that the NHL prepared an apology letter and I signed it.

Everyone in the hockey world knew I would never write a letter like the one I signed. But I didn't want to be fined or suspended, and I couldn't be sure what would happen if I refused to sign.

MY RELATIONSHIP WITH THE NHL office had been strained before I made those comments about Bettman.

During the 1993–94 season, I had been suspended twice, and one of those suspensions was completely unjustified in my opinion. I felt as if the NHL was targeting me.

At the start of the season, the NHL had sent league vice president Jim Gregory to Chicago to meet with me and to warn me that the league was not pleased with how I conducted myself on the ice.

I had kicked Pittsburgh's Ulf Samuelsson during the previous season and had thrown my helmet in the direction of an opposing player. Gregory's meeting with me was supposed to be an official warning.

He told me that league officials would be watching me, and if I had any more incidents, a suspension would surely follow.

As you can imagine, I was offended that someone from the NHL was trying to tell me how to play the game.

It's fair to say I was mouthy to Gregory. I didn't curse him or act disrespectfully but I made my feelings known.

"Don't ever tell me how to play," I told him as the meeting broke up.

What NHL officials didn't know was that I had already planned to tone things down in 1993–94 simply because I thought it was in the best interest of the team. Coach Darryl Sutter wanted us to be more disciplined.

To encourage myself to hold fast to my commitment, I bet a friend $500 that I wouldn't have a misconduct penalty during the entire 1993–94 season. One of the incentives for me to make that bet was that he was giving me 12–1 odds.

Those odds were appropriate because I had amassed 282 penalty minutes in 1992–93.

I believed I could win that bet.

Two weeks into the season, I had already lost it.

The NHL gave me a richly deserved four-game suspension after I amassed 51 penalty minutes and sucker-punched Hartford Whalers defenseman Adam Burt in a game at Chicago Stadium on October 14, 1993. I was fighting Brian Propp, and I abandoned that fight to help Brian Noonan, who was tangled up with Burt.

As I left the Propp scrap to go after Burt, I ended up dragging one of the linesmen with me on my back. However, linesmen Bernie DeGrace and Randy Mitton and referee Kerry Fraser all told NHL supplemental discipline czar Brian Burke that they didn't believe my misdeed constituted "abuse of officials."

I appreciated their honesty because I certainly had not intended to involve them in my battle.

That was statistically the wildest game of my career because I received a team-record 51 penalty minutes. My 37 minutes of penalties in the third period broke the previous team record of 32 minutes in a period, held jointly by Reggie Fleming and my former Blackhawks teammate Stu Grimson.

My rap sheet in that game included two game misconducts for instigating the fight with Propp and being the third man into the Noonan-Burt bout, and two 10-minute misconducts. Then there was my fighting major, plus a slashing call and a high-sticking call, plus another minor.

Obviously, Propp and I had some history going back to my days in Montreal, when I rammed his head into a stanchion.

"Chelios is a terrible person, the kind of guy who would stick your eye out and not care," Propp told the *Chicago Tribune* after the game.

Geez, Propp, don't pull your punches. Tell us how you really feel.

Blackhawks captain Dirk Graham answered Propp with this quote to the press: "Chris is a team-oriented person and what he does—right or wrong—he does for the team. I'll take Chris Chelios on my team every time and accept the way he is."

The Hartford skirmish had started when we were trying to kill a 5-on-3 power play. Whalers right wing Pat Verbeek tripped me right off the faceoff in front of Fraser. He didn't make the call.

Instead, he just laughed at me. Incensed by the no-call, I stirred up trouble for myself.

In that hearing with Burke, I laid out my concern that I was not being treated fairly by NHL officials. Obviously I had a bit of lawlessness in my game, and I deserved most of the penalties I received. But I was also being called for crimes I didn't commit, and some of my opponents were getting away with murder against me.

In the 1992–93 season, I was given a misconduct penalty for just being on the ice when something broke out. I was told the misconduct was for my "intent."

"That's like being put in jail for thinking about robbing a bank," I told *Tribune* sportswriter Mike Kiley.

Burke said he would review my complaint about referees giving me unfair treatment.

When the four-game suspension was handed down, the press reported it as being for abuse of officials. But in the hearing, Burke's aggravation with me was over the sucker-punch.

Whether I was suspended for the punch or for pulling the linesman along didn't truly matter as much as the fact that I was going to miss four games.

We had lost that Hartford game 6–2 and Sutter wasn't pleased with my lack of discipline. You have to remember the Blackhawks had been knocked out of the playoffs in the first round in both 1991 and 1993 because we took too many penalties.

"Chelios' lack of preparation highlighted the team's lack of preparation," Sutter told the *Tribune*. "You've got to have discipline from your top players."

My second suspension that season, coming in February for my alleged eye gouge to Vancouver Canucks defenseman Dana

Murzyn, is the one that still gnaws at me to this day because I was innocent of all charges.

The hearing with Burke didn't go well. Pulford had told me not to say anything to Burke, but we ended up in a "fuck you" argument. At one point, Pulford was physically trying to calm me down.

Burke agreed that the video was inconclusive, but said he was basing his four-game suspension on the testimony of linesman Shane Heyer, who said he saw me do it. My theory was that no one actually saw it, but Heyer reacted to the Canucks' view of the events.

When we looked at the video there was no linesman looking in my direction. When Heyer heard players yelling, he turned and saw me and probably concluded I was guilty. You can see that Heyer wasn't looking at me. What really occurred on the play was that Murzyn eye-gouged *me*. I had a scratch from my eye down my cheek.

Referee Bill McCreary admitted that he didn't see the play, which had started with me slashing Trevor Linden along the boards.

When Burke suspended me, it felt as if my belief that the league was targeting me had been confirmed. It really felt like I had been convicted of a crime that I didn't commit with absolutely no evidence.

"I think that's pretty harsh," Sutter told the media. "If that's a four-game suspension, there should be a lot of them."

Going down quietly is not in my nature. I told the media I felt the officials were biased against me.

"It's pretty obvious which referees don't like us," I said. "We've had problems with guys like McCreary, Fraser, and [Denis]

Morel. If they don't like us, they shouldn't be doing our games. When a game's over, it's supposed to be over. But some referees and linesmen hold a grudge against us. We make their job harder because we play physically, and they don't like it."

In hindsight, I was clearly a difficult player for McCreary, Fraser, Morel, and the rest of the officials to referee. It's an insanely tough job to maintain control over a bunch of hockey players, and on balance I got what I deserved.

At that time in my career, I was making $1.1 million, so I lost more than $80,000 for those two suspensions.

What I can say is that those two suspensions did cure me of my wayward ways. I didn't enjoy losing the money, and I felt terrible because I was letting down my team by not being able to play. Plus, Sutter worked overtime to make sure I felt like a complete asshole for putting our team in a bad position.

If you look at my penalty minute totals after those two suspensions, they declined significantly.

Take away the record-setting 51-minute game I posted against Hartford and I totaled just 161 penalty minutes in 1993–94. That's a sharp decline from the 282 penalty minutes I registered in 1992–93.

Over the next 15 years, I never had more than 151 penalty minutes. In several seasons, I had fewer than 100 minutes.

Detroit coach Scotty Bowman hated penalties taken after the whistle, and I respected him enough to make sure I followed his directive.

Red Wings coach Mike Babcock had the same disdain for undisciplined penalties. Although I always tried to respect his wishes, I did get into trouble a couple of times.

In 2003–04, I suffered a shoulder injury in the playoffs on a hit by Calgary Flames forward Oleg Saprykin.

Because the 2004–05 season was lost to a lockout, I didn't get a chance to even the score until a preseason game in 2004–05 when Saprykin was playing for the Phoenix Coyotes. By then, Babcock was our coach.

When Saprykin bumped goalie Chris Osgood, it was the only excuse I needed to attack him. I ended up getting tossed from the game, and Babcock was not amused.

"If you do those kinds of things you are going to be watching the game from the stands," Babcock told me.

I promised it wouldn't happen again, and then early in the regular season I ended up firing a puck down the ice after the play had stopped. I was angry about something and I was assessed a 10-minute misconduct. I distinctly remember sitting in the penalty box wondering whether Babcock would ever play me again.

Fortunately, I was able to survive Babcock's wrath after that incident. But honestly, my anger over the wrongful suspension over the Murzyn incident has never subsided.

That's not to say I disliked Burke as a person. We have a lot in common when it comes to the way we believe hockey should be played. He appreciates physical hockey. He is outspoken, the same way I am on occasion.

Burke was critical of my actions during the hearing, but when I was leaving the office he shook my hand and said he loved the way I played. He said he wished I had been on his team.

However, as much as I liked Burke, I didn't like him in that job. He had the wrong temperament for the position. He was too quick to judge and he liked to argue. Once the hearing started, I had the feeling that no matter what I said it wasn't going to impact his ruling.

Not long after the second suspension, Burke and I both ended up as competitors at Mark Messier's charity fishing tournament near the Queen Charlotte Islands in British Columbia. When I was in high school, I fished all of the time. At night, my buddy Russell Lowell and I used to go fishing for rainbow trout near San Diego. My mom would fry them up for us in the morning. I enjoyed fishing, but never had much of a chance to do it when I was playing in the NHL.

So I was happy to attend this charity fishing event, but I went out of my way to avoid Burkie.

"So you are still not talking to me?" said Burke, who is not one to let sleeping dogs lie.

I wanted to continue to be mad at him, but I had won a pile of money in the fishing tournament and I was too happy to be mad.

Messier's tournament allowed people to bid on celebrities to be their fishing partner. One of Messier's friends, a New York lawyer named Barry, had won the auction to be my partner. Sorry to say I don't know what he paid for that privilege.

Whenever I've been a prize for an auction at a charity event, I always believed it was my obligation to make sure the "winner" had a good time.

So, the night before this tournament I decided to take Barry out on the town. Drinks were consumed. The only thing I remember about the night was that comedian/actor Tom Arnold had been hired as the entertainment and he was hilarious talking about his ex-wife Roseanne Barr.

I was trying to be a good host to Barry, but we did too much celebrating and I slept through my wake-up call the next morning. As a result, I missed the charter plane that was flying us to the first location.

Not wanting to let Barry down, I chartered a helicopter to fly me up to the fishing area. When I showed up, Barry was also feeling the impact of our night of revelry. He was throwing up as I boarded the boat.

All of the participants had thrown in $5,000 each and most of the money went to charity, with some being set aside for prize money.

Despite missing a half day of fishing, I caught a 26-pound salmon and Barry landed an even larger fish. We won $25,000 each for having the biggest combined catch of the day.

That salmon is mounted on the wall at my restaurant in Detroit.

With all of the fun I was having at the tournament, I couldn't stay mad at Burke. But I still bring up my wrongful suspension to him at every opportunity.

When Burke named me to the U.S. staff for the 2010 Olympics in Vancouver, I brought up the 16-year-old suspension.

"I guess we will have to get along here," I said.

He probably thought that comment would be all he heard about the subject. He should have known better. I'm stubborn when it comes to matters of principle.

We were out together one night in Vancouver and I brought it up again before an exasperated Burke tried to get the last word in on the subject.

"Let's say we were wrong—I'm not saying we were—but let's say we were," Burke said. "If we were wrong, you got a four-game suspension you didn't deserve. But it probably made up for a four-game suspension you should have gotten when we didn't catch you."

I had to laugh at that one.

But that doesn't mean I won't stop harassing him every time I see him.

15

The Worst of Times

After more than three decades of making a living in the NHL, it's difficult for me to decide which moment was the best of my career.

But it is painfully easy for me to identify the lowest moments of my life.

Watching my younger sister, Gigi, die from cancer in 2000 at the age of 36 hit me harder than anything that ever happened to me in the NHL.

After being diagnosed with breast cancer, my sister battled the disease for more than a decade before it overwhelmed her body. Twice she went into remission, only to have the cancer return. During her 10-year battle, I would say she had six good years.

Fortunately, my NHL career provided me the financial resources to help her as much as I could. When we exhausted our medical options in the United States, we took her to Mexico to be treated with drugs that had not yet been approved in the U.S.

I spent countless hours on the phone with doctors, trying to sort through our options.

One summer, I accompanied Gigi south of the border. It was a depressing experience. All of the patients were in the advanced stages of cancer. You go there to find hope, but you don't feel very hopeful in a large room filled with critically ill patients hooked up to intravenous bags.

Obviously, those treatments didn't cure my sister's cancer. But they seemed to strengthen her enough to resume her chemo and radiation treatments in the U.S. In hindsight, I believe the treatments in Mexico extended her life. In those situations, you simply do whatever you can to help.

Before my sister died, I vowed to myself that I was going to maintain a strong bond with my family. My sister's death at such a young age strengthened that resolve.

When Gigi was 15, she ran away from home. We didn't know where she was for a year. We only found her because she had been hit by a car in Los Angeles and the hospital called us.

Once she came back into our lives, Gigi and I became much closer. She worked for me at Cheli's Chili Bar in Chicago. That's what seemed to keep her going.

Our family was dealing with the final stage of Gigi's illness when I was breaking up with the Blackhawks in 1999.

I've wondered if her struggles affected my thinking at that time. Watching someone close to you wilt away causes anger. Did that cloud my judgment? I'll never know. As previously mentioned, a significant reason I agreed to play for the Red Wings was because I knew it would be easier to get back to Chicago to visit Gigi.

I was in Red Wings training camp when I received the call that I needed to get back to Chicago immediately. Fortunately, I made it in time to talk to Gigi one last time before she lost consciousness and passed away.

Anyone who has gone through grief like that knows it is impossible to convey how devastating it is. On one hand, you want to go right back to work to regain some normalcy in your life. On the other hand, it doesn't seem fair to you that you keep living your life while your loved one is gone.

I HOPED THAT I would never experience grief like that again. Unfortunately, I encountered more tragedy in 2007 when a 17-year-old former employee came into my sports bar in Detroit and stabbed two of my employees to death.

It was just after 8:00 in the morning, and I was on the phone with my manager Megan Soroka three minutes before she was attacked and killed.

Restaurant managers know they have to be extra cautious on January 2; criminals know there is usually plenty of cash in the safe because no bank deposits are made on New Year's Day.

While we were talking on the phone, I asked Megan to see if the staff had found Detroit center Pavel Datsyuk's cell phone. I had hosted a party for my teammates at the bar, and Datsyuk had left without picking up his phone.

She said she had Datsyuk's phone but had to go because she heard a commotion downstairs. She said she would call me right back, but the call never came.

What we now know is that the noise she heard was our cook Mark Barnard being stabbed to death. Megan was attacked as she went down to investigate. Knowing where our cameras were, the former employee killed Megan and Mark in blind spots. But he is seen on video in the bar when he clearly had no business being there. DNA evidence was later found on clothes taken from his home.

Another employee was in the restaurant at the time of the murders, but he didn't respond when the attacker yelled for him to come out. Again, the murderer was trying to avoid the cameras.

Megan's and Mark's bodies were discovered a short time later. About $8,000 was missing from the safe.

That was the same day that Steve Yzerman's jersey was going to be retired by the Red Wings. As I was preparing for the morning skate, I received the call saying I needed to come to the bar immediately.

The killer was quickly identified thanks to our surveillance system. He had been fired twice from the restaurant, and we had given him $50 as severance the second time.

We have never understood why he killed anyone; neither Megan nor Mark had made the decision to fire him. And if he was simply after the money, he could have easily overpowered Megan and just left. Why did he have to kill them? You think about all of these things when something like this happens. Is there anything I could have done differently?

I missed the next couple of Red Wings games attending the funerals for people who were like family members to me. Megan had been my manager for seven years. She loved working in downtown Detroit.

At the trial, I had to testify that the teenager on the video tape was indeed my former employee. It was the most uncomfortable situation I've ever been in. While I was testifying on the stand, this kid was trying to stare me down.

What I wanted to do was walk over to the defense table, pull him across it, and pound the shit out of him.

Instead, the judge gave him life with no chance of parole. Unfortunately, it doesn't bring Megan and Mark back to us and their families.

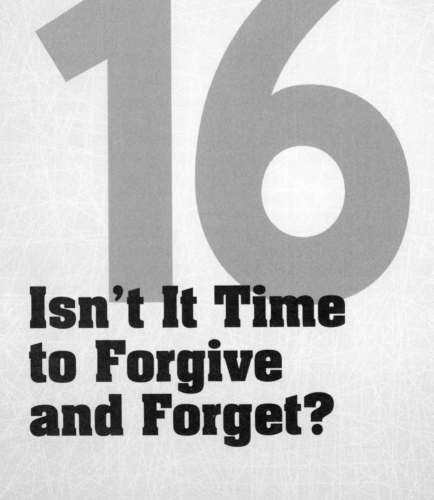

16

Isn't It Time to Forgive and Forget?

Whenever I played on the road during my NHL career, fans always treated me as if I was Public Enemy No. 1. I was always the villain.

Fans yelled at me, cursed at me, taunted me, and threw all manner of items at me. Given all of the shenanigans I was involved with at the end of games, I probably earned most of the boos I received.

Time has not healed all of the wounds in some arenas. At the 2011 draft in St. Paul, a couple of inebriated fans were so obnoxious with their heckling that I vowed I wouldn't attend future drafts out of courtesy to our scouts. They shouldn't have to try to debate the merits of potential draft picks while a couple of guys in the front row are cussing at me for plays I made a decade before.

It's been four years since I retired and I have been wondering whether enough time has passed for fans to forgive my playing style. But when I saw the 2014 draft was going to be in Philadelphia, I decided to give it another year.

I can't imagine Philadelphia fans giving me a free pass.

During my playing career, I sometimes had to tip my cap to the most creative fans who came up with clever taunts or signs. Some of them even made me laugh. My all-time favorite was one that read CHELIOS, YOU ARE EVEN UGLIER THAN MIKE RICCI.

Once, during a playoff series in Edmonton, a young man of Middle Eastern descent held up a sign that read YOU OWE MY MOTHER CHILD SUPPORT.

When I skated by him, I yelled, "I'm Greek!"

At some point, you realize as a professional athlete that you may as well just play along. One guy in Columbus created a different insulting sign every time I played there, and eventually I ended up meeting him and giving him an autograph.

The one opposing fan that I didn't like was the guy in Los Angeles who always wore a knit cap and would scream down at me as I walked through the tunnel to get to the ice. His rants were always over the top.

Usually, I was able to ignore what was said to me. But this guy did push my buttons to the point that I came very close to fighting him. Tony Danza and I were at a boxing match in Los Angeles when I ran into the knit-cap-wearing Kings fan. Imagine my surprise when the guy started screaming at me just like he did at Kings games. I got mad enough to show him what I thought of his bush league antics.

We were about to square off when security guards came flying in from every direction. They stopped the fight before punches were thrown.

It would have been one thing to only be heckled and hated when I was in uniform, but sadly that was not the case. Some fans thought nothing of insulting and screaming at me on the street, in restaurants, and especially in bars. Because fans viewed me as Darth Vader on skates, they seemed to believe it was perfectly acceptable to yell at me no matter where we happened to be located.

It was always trouble if I was at any event where alcohol was being served. The more fans drank, the more brave they became about telling me what they thought of my playing style.

When my children grew old enough to play travel hockey, it was often uncomfortable for me to go with them, especially if those tournaments were in Canada.

It always amazed me how many people would hurl insults at me hoping that I would react in some fashion. My response was always to say nothing. People would be surprised when I wouldn't react, but I was never going to allow myself to become involved in a war of words if my family was around.

WHILE I WAS WILLING to accept being viewed as a bad guy in Canada or NHL rinks around North America, it was difficult for me to accept the fact that I was persona non grata in my hometown.

Never would I have guessed that some people in Chicago would still hate me because I allowed myself to be traded to Detroit back in 1999.

It's been 15 years, but some Chicago fans still have not forgiven me.

I certainly understood how they felt at the time of the trade. The first few times I came back as a member of the Red Wings, the wound was still raw. But it was disappointing when it became clear that some people were still holding a grudge more than a decade later.

On December 17, 2010, a few months after I retired as a player, the Blackhawks honored me as part of their heritage night celebrations.

A good number of fans booed me as I tried to give my speech.

I can't say I was totally surprised. I had been back to Chicago many times through the years. My parents still live there. And it didn't matter if I was at Wrigley Field singing "Take Me Out to the Ball Game" or having dinner with friends at one of my favorite restaurants; it seemed like somebody always had something to say about what they viewed as the traitorous act I had committed many years before.

Frankly, I was saddened by the lack of forgiveness for many, many years. It bothered me because I've always been proud of my Chicago roots. My father has been a Blackhawks fan since 1956, the year before Bobby Hull joined the team. At one point, my mother had a homemade sweater that was half Blackhawks and half Red Wings.

When I was a young hockey player in Chicago, I wore No. 3 because I loved Blackhawks rough-and-tumble defenseman Keith Magnuson. Before every game in Chicago, he would step on the ice and do a hot lap. The fans loved him. He was fearless. He would fight anyone.

I had grown up on the South Side idolizing Chicago Bears linebacker Dick Butkus, who also played his sport up against the edge of the rules. Every Chicago kid in my era grew up loving Butkus. At the end of his career, his knees were killing him but he still got out there and played. He could hardly run but he was still a force.

If not for the fact that my children have now developed roots up in Michigan, I would be living in Chicago today.

The *Chicago Tribune* wrote a story about my parents' "torn loyalties" in 2009, and the writer noted that my mother was wearing a diamond necklace commemorating the Stanley Cups

I won with Montreal in 1986 and Detroit in 2002 and 2008. But below that necklace commemorating her son's successes she wore a gold Indian head.

In my parents' house, there's an old photograph of Chicago Stadium that was given to my father by Peter Wirtz, son of the late Bill Wirtz.

When Blackhawks team president John McDonough first talked to me about making the appearance at the United Center, I remember warning him that the fans were going to boo me.

He didn't believe it. My wife, Tracee, also tried to convince me that fans would respect the occasion. Since the Blackhawks had invited me to an event, she believed the fans would politely applaud.

And to be fair, the thawing of my relationship with fans in Chicago had started to occur by then. I had been treated quite well by Chicago Wolves fans in 2009–10. And the Wirtz family and the Blackhawks organization had treated me very well throughout my Red Wings years, and they had always taken care of my parents.

That said, I knew how passionate the fans in the building were. I didn't think it was time for a Chris Chelios celebration at the United Center.

I was right.

I had a speech prepared but I crumpled it up as the booing grew louder and louder. My wife was behind me and said, "Chris, be careful what you say."

Holding that microphone tight, I just said, "Let's let bygones be bygones, all right?"

I was embarrassed, mostly because my family was there. But I looked over and my family was taking it well. My daughter Caley was actually laughing her head off. But I glanced at my daughter Tara and I didn't like the look on her face. I could see she was disappointed by what was happening. She felt bad for me. At that point, there wasn't much that could be done.

It was a short speech. I handed the microphone to Jeremy Roenick and walked off the ice.

When the media asked me about the booing, I said I certainly understood the nature of the Chicago-Detroit rivalry and why fans still had negative feelings toward me. In their defense, some fans did cheer that night, and there would have been more boos had that event been held a couple of years earlier.

I did joke with the media that if any of the hecklers wanted to boo in my face, my sons Dean and Jake, my dad, and I would be waiting outside Gate 3-1/2.

You have to have a sense of humor about things like that.

IF I HAD TO do everything over again, would I still go to Detroit? After all, a couple of days before that trade was announced I had given a lengthy interview to the *Tribune* reporter in the back of a commercial airplane during which I stated unequivocally that I wanted to remain a Blackhawk for life.

But when the team wouldn't give me a contract extension, I had to do what was best for me and my family. At 37, I knew I could still play. I certainly didn't expect to play for another decade. But I was sure I could still play significant minutes for a good team.

Hawks GM Bob Murray thought I was approaching the end of my career, and I disagreed. If I had stayed with the Blackhawks, I would not have been doing what was best for my family.

Deep down, I think most people know that if they had been in my position in 1999, they would have done the same thing.

There are still fans in Chicago who refuse to forgive my decision to leave, and there probably always will be. But the situation has improved, especially since I was inducted into the Hall of Fame. It was almost as if that event reminded Chicago fans that I was still one of them.

Kid Rock is a Detroiter. Bruce Springsteen is a New Jerseyan.

And even though I'm living in Michigan, Chris Chelios is a Chicagoan.

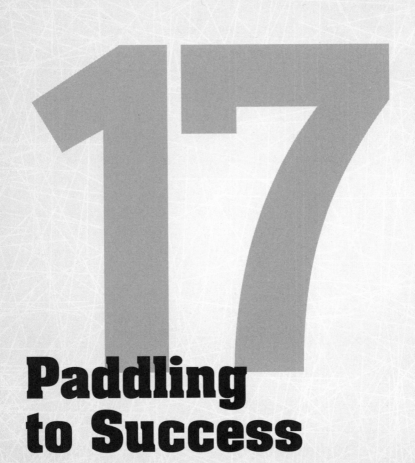

17

Paddling
to Success

As I write these words, I am 52 and weigh 187 pounds. I also weighed 187 pounds when I signed with the Montreal Canadiens 30 years ago.

People have asked me a million times over the years how I managed to play hockey at the highest level for so many years.

I wish I could say I had found a fountain of youth, but there was no secret formula that allowed me to play in the NHL until I was 47. I didn't plan to play for more than a quarter of a century. It just happened.

Undoubtedly, I benefited from a forgiving metabolism. But the primary reason I was able to play almost as long as Gordie Howe did is that I worked at maximizing my conditioning level before it was fashionable to do so. I treated my body as if I would need it a long while.

Being in excellent shape was a real advantage when I started playing in the NHL because athletes did not embrace year-round conditioning like they do today.

Bob Gainey was probably in the best shape of all of the Canadiens in that era, and that came simply from running. He didn't lift weights.

When the Canadiens had physical testing in training camp, the younger players such as Claude Lemieux, Mike McPhee,

Brian Skrudland, Patrick Roy, and I dominated because we had spent our off-season training.

Every NHL team had smokers in the 1980s when I started playing. Larry Robinson smoked, as did Pierre Mondou, Mario Tremblay, Ric Nattress, Chris Nilan, and a few others on the Canadiens. Coach Jacques Lemaire banned smoking from the dressing room, and kept moving the smokers farther and farther away. At one point, they could smoke in the wives' room and then I believe it was in the hallway. Finally, they had to leave the building.

Even into the 1990s, the NHL had smokers. Steve Larmer was one of the NHL's top wingers, and he smoked.

Thankfully, that was one vice I never had. I was always concerned about my body. I wanted to be quick and strong on my skates. As a general rule, the lighter I was the better I felt. During the regular season, I would maintain my weight around 187 or 188. If we went long into the playoffs, my weight would drop to closer to 180 because of the minutes I logged.

I never felt as if I was at a disadvantage against bigger players because I felt quick and strong at that weight.

Having a good metabolism helped me early in my career when I didn't have to pay attention to what I ate. I thought about what I was eating earlier in my career, but I had four kids. I would not order anything for myself if I took the kids out, but I would end up eating half their food. All parents know how that works; those fries at the bottom of the bag probably put four or five pounds per year on you if you aren't careful.

Early in my career I made good eating choices some days and bad choices other days. But when I made poor eating choices on any given day, I worked out twice as hard the following day.

Training to be the best athlete I could be is something I've done since my days in Moose Jaw. Back then, my training regimen was similar to a boxer's. I liked to run and work with the heavy bag.

My idea of what training should be changed dramatically when I went to Wisconsin and started working with assistant coach Grant Standbrook. He was in his forties back then, but he was in better physical shape than many of his players. He was ripped.

He could walk into our weight room and squat more than any player on our team. He was in crazy, twisted-steel shape.

The facilities at Wisconsin were so good that I felt like it was easy to stay well conditioned. Working on upper body strength was never part of my process. I couldn't even do a single chin up. My best bench press was probably only 240 pounds. I had never had a shoulder injury, so I never wanted to mess with that area of my body. I was always working on my leg strength and cardiovascular ability.

At Wisconsin, the tradition was for hockey players to run the stairs at Randall Stadium. Former NHL player Paul Ranheim had the record for most stairs run in a predetermined time. I wish I would have known that because I would have tried to beat his record when I was training there in the off-season.

Somewhere along the line another NHL player, Tom Laidlaw, said to me that "your strength all comes from your core," and that made sense to me.

Even as I grew older, I never deviated from my belief that I needed to keep my legs strong. At one point, my slap shot was timed at 100 mph. I didn't believe I needed any additional upper body strength.

Hand strength was one of my advantages. When we were tested on our grip strength, I was always miles ahead of everyone else. My father had taught me the tricks of arm wrestling when I was young, and I developed an impressive grip. At bars, I would look at a tough-looking guy in my weight class and bet him I could beat him in arm wrestling. A technique my dad taught me has worked for 40 years.

Guys who are my size do not often beat me in arm wrestling. When I grabbed guys, I always felt like I could hang on. That came in handy during my 63 NHL fights.

The last arm wrestling match I lost was to Rage Against the Machine bassist Tim Commerford. I felt as if I had him beat, but he pulled out and we had to restart. That's to my disadvantage, because I put so much strain on my elbow that I'm only good for one major battle per night.

Before the 1991 Canada Cup, I decided I wanted to try to beef up to see if it would help me. I worked on my upper body and pushed my weight up to 205.

I absolutely hated it. I felt like I couldn't move the way I wanted to move. It was as if my body wasn't strong enough to carry that much weight. It took me three weeks to lose the 17 pounds, and I decided then that I would stay around 187 for the rest of my career.

MY INTRODUCTION TO TRAINER T.R. Goodman was a matter of happenstance in the early 1990s. I was at a California gym working out with my friend, actor Tony Danza, when I spotted a trainer putting someone through a hardcore workout.

It looked like something I would like.

"What are you guys doing?" I asked Goodman.

"It's circuit training," he answered.

As it turned out, the athlete he was working with was NHL tough guy Alan May.

I asked whether I could join them the next day, and I liked it so much that I trained with Goodman in California for the better part of two decades.

I chose to work out at 6:00 AM because it forced me to be in bed at 9:00 PM. One of the reasons I bought a home in California was to get away from everyone in the summer so I could spend time with my family and stay disciplined in my training.

Honestly, after spending the day outside in California I couldn't stay up beyond 9:00 anyway. A day at the beach under the sun really drains you.

Here is what one of my one-hour training sessions would look like.

Jumping rope: 50 revolutions to build my endurance.

Close-grip press: To work my triceps, I gripped a 20-pound bar with 35-pound plates on each end. I pressed the bar until my arms, shoulder-length apart, were fully extended.

One-armed row: With my right leg back and left leg bent, I gripped a 45-pound dumbbell in my right hand and raised it until my elbow was at back level. I would do eight reps.

Dumbbell press: Lying on a bench, I gripped a 45-pound dumbbell in each hand. My arms would be bent at either side of my chest. I extended my arms, then lowered them to the sides of my chest. I would do eight reps to strengthen my chest and shoulders.

Dumbbell dead-lift: To strengthen my lower back, hamstrings, and calves, I gripped a pair of 35-pound dumbbells with my palms facing in. I bent at the waist, head up, knees slightly bent, and then straightened up completely. I would do eight reps.

Note that I wasn't working with heavy weights; again, I wasn't that interested in upper body strength. I just wanted to make sure my core and overall fitness were up to my standards, and the intensity and speed with which we worked out did the job.

As a rule, I would work with T.R. primarily in July and August. The first month would be stretching, which I hated, and heavy lifting to get to my max. The final three weeks were circuit training.

Around that time I became friends with surfer Laird Hamilton and fitness guru Don Wildman, who was the founder of Bally's Total Fitness. He's 80 now, and he finishes high in senior Olympic events every year. Those two guys pulled me into paddling and mountain bike riding.

Sometimes, I would take a 40-mile bike ride along the Pacific Coast Highway, then spend the afternoon paddle-surfing for 16 miles in the Pacific Ocean.

I would use the Hawaiian technique of standing on a 12-foot board while using a seven-foot oar. It's a challenging workout when you factor in the waves and wind. You use the paddle to balance yourself and steer. Paddling worked my legs, stomach, shoulders, and back. My son Dean or Laird would paddle with me.

On Mondays, Wednesdays, and Fridays, we would race on our bikes for one hour straight up the mountain. Tuesdays and

Thursdays were heavy weight days, followed by long bike rides. We might be riding up and down mountains for up to four hours; there are thousands of miles of trails. Because Wildman has been out there more than 20 years, he knows every inch of them.

To me, it was a thrill ride every time we went out. It was an adrenaline rush. It was dangerous. I fell so many times the summer I started riding, I was just lucky that I was never seriously hurt.

I went over the handlebars a few times but I never fell off the mountain. I saw other guys do that, mostly on the downhill, because they refused to reduce their speed. I never went full speed downhill because I always reminded myself that I had too much to lose.

If those guys broke their collarbone or blew out their knee, they would view their rehab as part of their training. But they weren't training for anything specific like I was.

Rage bassist Tim Commerford is an experienced mountain biker. But as a result of all that experience he has metal plates in his head. He recently broke his jaw and lost some teeth because these top bikers are crazy going down the hill. It scares me just watching them, the same way it did when those guys would jump off the highest cliffs at The Clam.

I couldn't fly down a hill in the middle of July because I was worried about how healthy I would be when the NHL season started in October.

What people don't know is that I actually had a falling out with Goodman and we stopped working together for a while.

I didn't like it when he started training Rob Blake because I felt it was a conflict of interest for him to train two elite defensemen who were competing against each other for the Norris Trophy and the recognition that came with it.

To me, it wasn't any different than an advertising agency taking on two clients from the same industry. Those companies are competing against each other for the same customers. An advertising agency wouldn't do work for both Chevrolet and Honda.

"I know you have to make a living," I said to T.R. one day. "But what chance do I have against Blake when he's 10 years younger than me and he's training the same way I do?"

Blake did win the Norris Trophy in 1998, and I really never got over that.

I felt Goodman should not have taken on another big-time defenseman as long as he had me as a client. He clearly had an impact on Blake, because Blake had been hampered by injuries until he started working with T.R.

The training methods I followed for so many years worked for me. I was always considered a well-conditioned athlete, and I didn't have too many major injuries.

If you look at the first 16 seasons of my career, I only missed a significant number of games in two seasons. I missed about half of a season in 1985–86 because of a knee injury, and then I missed 27 games in 1989–90.

I had three medial collateral ligament injuries, caused by hits from Quebec's Dale Hunter, Boston's Terry O'Reilly, and Colorado's Keith Jones.

For the most part, I would never miss more than 10 games in a season, and the games I would miss would result from broken bones.

I never really had any shoulder injuries, which might be a little strange, since for the majority of my career I wore Cooper shoulder pads that were designed to be used in the 1970s.

They once had belonged to Bobby Suter, Gary's brother, who had played on the 1980 Olympic gold medal team.

When Gary was traded to the Blackhawks in 1994, he had a pair and gave them to me. Incredibly to everyone around me, I wore them until I retired in 2008. Teammates always referred to them as "the rags" I wore. I changed the straps a few times, but the caps were still the same ones that Bobby Suter used.

I always felt like I was totally in tune with my own body, and was aware of everything that was feeling right or wrong with it. That's why I was pretty shocked during my first major physical with the Red Wings in 1999 when the doctor asked me when I had lost my anterior cruciate ligament (ACL).

I had no idea what he was talking about. Upon reflection, I remembered an incident I had with my knee back in Chicago but the doctor there never picked it up in the physical. I had torn the ACL clean off but my legs were so strong that they were able to support my knee without it.

Since it wasn't bothering me, I decided not to have any surgery. Today, I'm paying for it. The little movement kept grinding and grinding until it created a hole in my cartilage. It started to give out on me.

During the last three or four years of my career, it affected my training. The harder I trained the more that knee hurt. Eventually, I decided to stop training that knee and just figured I'd gut it out as long as I could.

ANOTHER REASON I WAS able to avoid injuries and play as long as I did was my approach to fighting. I was a competent fighter for someone my size, particularly in the early years when you could jump guys and get an edge on them.

But when I fought bigger guys or heavyweights, such as Bob Probert or Derian Hatcher, I fought to survive. I fought smart.

Often I went into fights not believing I could win but instead wanting to protect myself. I just wanted to avoid getting hurt or getting embarrassed.

No matter how smart or tough you think you are, you put yourself at risk anytime you get into a fight. When I fought Hatcher in 1995, I didn't know much about him. He had a cast on his hand and could only drop one glove. While we were locked up, Shane Churla came along and sucker-punched me. He ended up receiving a four-game suspension. That was little consolation to me at the time.

Self-preservation was also on my mind when I fought Probert. I was with Chicago then and Probert had hit my teammate Jocelyn Lemieux.

After wrestling Probert down I had him vulnerable, but before I threw a punch I thought to myself, *I'd better not do this.*

We started to tussle and then he just started laughing at me. Probert was an honest fighter. I remember he once had a chance to destroy Jeremy Roenick but he didn't do it. He knew J.R. was no match for a guy like him. Almost no one was.

It seemed like Probert tried to break my neck once, hitting me from behind, but I deserved it because I had done something to Steve Yzerman. Probert always stood up for his teammates, no matter what.

Larry Playfair, who played for the Los Angeles Kings and Buffalo Sabres, absolutely killed me in a fight once. I grabbed him because he was messing with our goalie and he hit me so hard on the top of the head that he chipped two teeth. Playfair was a good guy; he actually apologized through his brother Jimmy for that hit.

I DIDN'T PLAN TO play in the NHL for as long as I did. I just took things one season at a time, especially once I hit my forties. My fitness certainly played a role in my ability to continue playing, as did the fact that I wasn't logging heavy minutes late in my career. That wasn't by choice, but in hindsight Mike Babcock's decision not to play me as much as I would have liked might have added a season or two to my run.

Gordie Howe played until he was 52, and I used to tell him not to worry; his NHL record of being the oldest player in NHL history was safe.

But to be perfectly honest, I never ruled out the possibility that I would continue playing into my fifties. My body was holding up well enough for me to survive, and I never lost my desire to keep playing.

When I left the Red Wings, I wasn't sure I wanted to retire. I had three different opportunities to play for a Russian team in the Kontinental Hockey League. The only reason I didn't go was because of family considerations. Russia was too far away. Their season started in September, and training camp would have been held in August. I also didn't want to give up my summer.

That's when I decided to sign with the Chicago Wolves in the American Hockey League, and that turned out to be a great

258 • Chris Chelios

experience. The organization treated me well and the fans were exceptionally nice to me. It was also so great to be playing at home again.

On the ice, I was plus-34 with five goals and 22 points in 46 games. My level of play was strong enough to make me glad I did it. I certainly didn't feel like I was stealing somebody's spot or that I was hurting the team by being out there.

My AHL opponents were respectful to the point that it sometimes bordered on embarrassing. I found myself not playing as physical as I used to because no one was playing physical against me, except for one guy. Francis Lessard, a 230-pound tough guy on the San Antonio Rampage, nailed me with an elbow and ended up being suspended for three games by the AHL.

The playoffs were a different story. Every opponent dialed up the hostility and the competition seemed more like the hockey I was used to. I had some quality battles with Dallas Stars prospect Jamie Benn, who is now an NHL star.

My brief promotion from the Chicago Wolves to the Atlanta Thrashers in 2009–10 gave me my 26th NHL season to tie Gordie Howe's record.

Maybe I should not have accepted the call-up because I wasn't in NHL-ready shape, not by my standards anyway.

I had gone to the 2010 Olympics to work for USA Hockey, and I hadn't been training properly to return to the NHL. So I was surprised when Thrashers general manager Don Waddell called me and offered me another chance to play in the NHL.

In my first game with the Thrashers, I made a mistake against the Columbus Blue Jackets and cost us an important goal. I appeared in seven games, played a total of about 78 minutes, and recorded no points, and the Thrashers didn't win any of those games. It was disappointing because the Thrashers were fighting for a playoff spot. They didn't make it, finishing five points out of the eighth spot in the Eastern Conference.

One reason Waddell wanted me in Atlanta was to mentor Zach Bogosian, but I only played part of one game with him.

If I had started the season with Atlanta, I'm convinced I could have helped the team. Had I started with the team in October, or even if I would have been called up while I was playing regularly with the Wolves, I would have been in better condition. I believe I could have been a significant contributor had I been on the team start to finish.

Today, I am the same age that Howe was when he played his last NHL game. Do I feel like I could still be playing professional hockey? I can't answer for sure, but I think it's possible. I believe I would still be capable of playing in one of the better European leagues.

I certainly haven't lost my competitive edge. Just ask the guys out on the mountain bike trails.

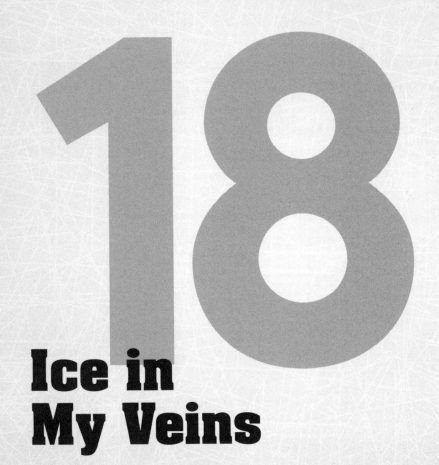

18

Ice in My Veins

I f you were one of the few people in the world to see the Hollywood flop *Waterworld*, you will remember that the Kevin Costner character had to remain on the ocean to live.

When I contemplate my future, that film comes to mind, because I feel as if I need to stay on the ice if I want to continue to work in hockey.

Unlike most former players, my interest is in coaching, not in team management or broadcasting. I am a player at heart, and I've worked with enough players to know that I enjoy the teaching side of the game.

I guess that means I think more like my former Blackhawks teammate Darryl Sutter than my former Red Wings teammate Steve Yzerman.

Around the hockey world I do see far more examples of ex-teammates wearing suits and ties than whistles. Yzerman worked under Detroit general manager Ken Holland for a while, and then became the GM of the Tampa Bay Lightning. Brendan Shanahan went straight from being a player to a league management position, and now he's the president of the Toronto Maple Leafs.

Luc Robitaille, who played on Detroit's 2002 Stanley Cup team with me, is a team president in Los Angeles. Former Red

Wings center Sergei Fedorov is a general manager for a team in the Kontinental Hockey League. Kris Draper is working under Ken Holland in Detroit.

Even Brett Hull was a general manager for a while in Dallas, and now is working for the St. Louis Blues.

My buddy Jeremy Roenick is an NBC analyst. Even my old USA teammates are moving into management. Bill Guerin is a member of the Pittsburgh Penguins' management team, and Doug Weight is now an assistant general manager with the New York Islanders.

But the idea of being a general manager is unappealing to me. Maybe I'm too much of a union guy at heart. I never want to be in the position of making decisions about players' long-term futures.

In my current job as advisor to hockey operations in Detroit, I work with the team's top prospects on our American Hockey League affiliate in Grand Rapids, Michigan. I drive up from the Detroit area for practices and get on the ice with the guys.

I enjoy my work and it feels as if I'm making a difference. When young players struggle, I know what to say because I have been in their skates before. I know what it is like when you are unsure of yourself.

In today's game, we identify potential stars early and many kids come into professional hockey brimming with confidence. All they have known in their careers is success. They don't know what to do when they hit the wall or a prolonged slump or discover that every player at this level is as fast, tough, and skilled as they are.

Because of the path I followed to get to the top, I experienced the self-doubt they are dealing with.

When I played at Moose Jaw, and Wisconsin, and for the U.S. Olympic team, and early in my career in Montreal, I wasn't sure I had what it took to be a top NHL player. During the 2014 Stanley Cup Final between the New York Rangers and Los Angeles Kings, L.A. coach Darryl Sutter said I was the best defenseman he ever coached. It was nice of him to say that. But I'm confident that Jacques Lemaire wouldn't put me in the top five.

When I played for Lemaire, he had to work with me every day to get me to the point where I was helping my team more than I was hurting it. Those are the memories I draw on to help my players in Grand Rapids. Since I didn't play in the minors before I went to the Canadiens, it took me a while to figure out what worked and what didn't. I'm trying to impart that knowledge to Detroit's prospects before they arrive in the NHL.

The only question I have about coaching is whether I want to commit the time necessary to do it on a full-time basis.

Right now, I'm a part-time coach working two or three days a week. A full-time coaching job requires around-the-clock devotion. You get to the rink early in the morning to break down game films and you are at the office late at night figuring out how you are going to beat your next opponent.

Holland I have had more than one conversation about whether that's what I want to do with my life. He believes I could step in now as an assistant coach at the NHL level.

But I love being with my family. I like my free time. The fact that my current job gave me the opportunity to see my sons, Jake and Dean, play hockey at Michigan State was very important to me. Now, I go to Northwestern to watch my daughters, Caley and Tara, play lacrosse. (Coincidentally, the lacrosse coach at

Northwestern just happens to be the sister of my former Chicago Blackhawks teammate Tony Amonte.)

IT'S BEEN SUGGESTED THAT another reason I haven't fully committed to coaching is that I haven't completely abandoned the idea of playing again.

When I was an assistant coach for a U.S. team at the Deutschland Cup international tournament in November 2011, I brought my gear with me just in case someone got injured.

My sons are now in pro hockey, and the idea that I might be able to play with my sons for a European team has been floating around for the past couple of seasons. Legendary Gordie Howe was the oldest player in NHL history, and he was able to play long enough to skate with his sons, Mark and Marty, in the now-defunct World Hockey Association. I think some people just connect the dots and think that as the second-oldest player in NHL history, I might want to play with my sons professionally.

I would be lying if I said that it had not crossed my mind.

At this point, it would be practical to point out again that I'm 52, the same age Gordie Howe was when he scored his last goal in the NHL for the Hartford Whalers.

Based on what I know about European hockey, I'm confident that I could achieve a high enough conditioning level to play over there.

But it is not likely to happen for a variety of reasons. First, Jake and Dean want to see what they can do in North American pro hockey. Second, I wouldn't go unless my wife believed it made sense for the entire family to come with me, and I'm not sure I could convince her of that.

Plus, I've started to spend more time managing my Cheli's Chili Bar down near Comerica Park. I'm actually signing the checks and paying more attention to the place that is a destination before and after Detroit Tigers games.

We don't offer a five-star menu, but we have good food at reasonable prices. We've made strides in establishing ourselves as a place that is attractive to everyone, including families. It's my name on the front door and I want to make sure it's managed properly.

Finally, I do enjoy what I'm doing now, and I wouldn't want to be disloyal to my current employer. The Red Wings have been very good to me.

My official comment about the possibility of playing with my sons is that I refuse to say it will never happen.

The last time I said something would never happen, it came back to bite me. I said I would never play for the Red Wings, and we know how that turned out. I'm not going to use the word *never* again when it comes to predicting what might happen in the future.

19
Riding the Wave

When I was informed that I had been elected to the Hockey Hall of Fame in 2013, it was hard for me to believe. Not because I was too humble to realize what I had accomplished in the game of hockey, but because I couldn't believe I'd had a chance to play in the first place.

In my mind, I had no business making the National Hockey League, let alone the Hall of Fame.

At 17, Larry Robinson, Denis Potvin, and Raymond Bourque were planning to go to the NHL. At 17, I was planning to go to the beach. Playing in the NHL wasn't in my game plan. I played hockey because I enjoyed the sport, not because I was trying to become an NHL player. People who lived in San Diego didn't dream about playing in the NHL.

Most of my surfing buddies thought I was a bit odd because I enjoyed playing late-night hockey in the adult beer-and-pizza leagues at the San Diego House of Ice.

I never thought about my future when I was a teenager. It's a Greek thing. You live today and enjoy it, and you worry about tomorrow when tomorrow comes.

When Bobby Parker gave me the telephone number of the coach in Moose Jaw, I didn't rush home to call him. I stuck the number in the glove compartment of Russell Lowell's car and didn't think about it for a couple of days.

Today's hockey players are committing to colleges when they are freshmen in high school. Some players have agents when they are 15. By 16, kids are identified as potential first-round draft picks.

But it never crossed my mind that I would have a career in hockey. No one in the NHL knew that I was alive until I landed in Moose Jaw.

Ultimately, I know that it was my hard work that landed me in the Hall of Fame. But that doesn't mean I can't marvel at the unlikelihood of the journey that took me from teenage beach bum delinquent to Hockey Hall of Famer. If I hadn't met Bobby Parker, or if I hadn't called Larry Billows, or if he hadn't liked me, I never would have gotten off that beach.

WHEN THE CALL CAME from the Hall of Fame, I just shook my head, because I knew I had been both lucky and good to be awarded such an honor.

The next thing I did was start thinking about the party I was going to throw in Toronto on my induction weekend.

About 100 close friends accepted my invitation. Four former teammates from my youth teams in Chicago even showed up.

Wayne Gretzky called and offered to host the party at his restaurant the night before the induction. Two days earlier, I had scheduled another party at former Montreal teammate Shayne Corson's Tappo Wine Bar and Restaurant.

I remember sitting back and seeing Kid Rock up front singing, and NBA star Michael Jordan, model Cindy Crawford, and Brett

Hull sitting at tables having a great time. I remember thinking *I'm never going to have a better party than this one.*

Honestly, it surprised me that Jordan came. MJ has a hectic schedule, to say the least. But when I called and invited him, he immediately said he was coming. "We've been through a lot together," he said. "I'll be there."

Gretzky kept telling me that he couldn't make the induction because of his schedule. He and I have been friends for a long time. He kept apologizing for not being able to make it. He said he felt terrible about it but hoped I had a good time at his restaurant.

Then I looked up and he and his wife, Janet, and other members of their family were walking in the door. Gretzky was laughing his ass off and was overjoyed that he'd pulled one over on me. He joked to the press later that during my induction speech he was going to count all of the times I whacked him with my stick.

TENNIS LEGEND JOHN McENROE, as well as actors Cuba Gooding Jr., Tony Danza, John McGinley, Jeremy Piven, D.B. Sweeney, and John Cusack were all in Toronto for my induction. Those are some of the people that Danza and I have dubbed the Malibu Mob. We usually spend a lot of time together in the summer. Taverna Tony, a Greek restaurant in Malibu, is one of our hangouts.

I joined that circle of friends after buying a home in Malibu, California, 22 years ago. I chose to live out there because it gave me a couple of months every year where my family would be my priority.

Malibu is a small community, and it wasn't long before we started meeting all of the famous people who lived there. McEnroe bought the late Johnny Carson's house and has been living there for many years. Actress Shirley MacLaine also lives in my neighborhood. (I don't know if she lived in Malibu in her previous lives.) Surfer Laird Hamilton also lives nearby.

Eight years ago, my original realtor called to say that he remembered I had originally wanted to live in the Malibu community of Paradise Cove, and that he knew of a house for sale that had not even been officially listed.

Immediately, I drove over to the real estate office. When I was told about the property and where it was, I said I would take it at the asking price. Knowing the home values in the area, I quickly surmised that it was bargain.

The home owner's realtor balked at presenting the offer before the listing went up, saying she had two other people wanting to look at the property.

My realtor immediately got into her face and said she had an ethical obligation to present my offer to the seller, regardless of other people wanting to see the house. An offer is an offer, particularly when it is for the seller's asking price.

Clearly, his realtor wanted to encourage a bidding war. Obviously, I was opposed to that happening.

We could hear her talking to her seller, and explaining who the other potential buyers were.

"The man with the offer is a hockey player from Michigan," she said.

He must have asked my name, because the realtor said, "Chris Chelios."

Shortly thereafter, she said simply that the seller had accepted my offer.

As it turned out, the seller was someone I had met at a party with Kid Rock. He had made millions in the software industry and was a hockey fan. On the night we met, he had been partying too hard and was riding me mercilessly. He even picked on me for having a big nose.

But he made up for that by selling me his home, which came with a beach house. It has since tripled in value. (Sadly, I never got a chance to thank him, because six months after the sale he died of a heart attack. He was only 46.)

When I told Tracee about the new house, her first response was that we couldn't afford it. But I convinced her we would be fine because our existing house would sell quickly.

We ended up selling it to Jeremy Piven, who still lives there today.

It seems as if most everyone in Malibu has been to my home at one time or another, either for my Stanley Cup parties or other events.

My home is on a public beach, so my Stanley Cup parties have ended up with 400 guests at them because people just show up.

At the 2008 Stanley Cup party, we launched the day by taking the Stanley Cup to Coogie's Beach Café for breakfast. Director and actor Rob Reiner was there, and he came over and had his picture taken with the Cup. That was just the start of the celebrity fest.

Once we got to the beach, the Malibu Mob was there, along with Gretzky, Igor Larionov, Kid Rock, tennis player Jennifer Capriati, actor David Spade, plus my Red Wings teammates Darren McCarty, Jiri Hudler, and Dan Cleary. It was quite a day.

Kid Rock performed. Everyone who showed up that day came away knowing they had been at a real party.

One rule I have at my Malibu home is that no one is allowed to discuss religion or politics. As I've written, I have no patience for either, and in my house, you play by my rules.

That rule sometimes comes in handy, because I have close friends who are quite conservative and others who are quite liberal. For example, my buddies Kid Rock and Pearl Jam's Eddie Vedder are on opposite ends of the political spectrum.

Vedder and I had a strange first meeting. In the early 1990s when I was hanging out with Chicago Bulls star Dennis Rodman, I was at a party and saw this guy staring at me like he was trying to size me up.

It bugged me to the point that I asked a cop who the guy was. He said it was Vedder, which surprised me. He looked bigger and different on stage.

I went up and introduced myself, and he said he was sure he knew me from somewhere but couldn't figure out where.

"I'm a hockey player," I said.

"Nope, that's not it," he said. "I've never seen a hockey game."

We talked for a while and quickly realized that both of us had started out in Chicago and ended up living in San Diego at the same time. Vedder was also a surfer, and we were riding the waves in the same areas. We figure we crossed paths on the beach somewhere, although we can't be sure we ever actually met. We have been close friends since that party.

Regardless of their political views, my celebrity friends have always gotten along, except for the time Kid Rock started talking politics with the liberal John Cusack.

They went at it like they were on a cable news show. They argued until they both ran out of steam. It was comical.

"I don't know how you can be friends with that guy," Cusack told me.

The truth is I'm friends with Kid Rock because he's a great guy, and I'm friends with Cusack because he's a great guy. I don't much care about their politics.

That's when I instituted the rule of no political or religious debate in my house. No exceptions. Since then, Cusack has looked beyond Kid Rock's political agenda and sees him as a fascinating person. They get along famously.

If you meet Kid Rock in person, it's hard for you to believe he's the same guy you see on stage. Just like some athletes are different people on the field, Kid Rock is a different man on stage. He has a stage presence that is impossible to describe. I've seen him perform live about 30 times. He's not one of those artists who has to be alone with his thoughts before he performs.

One night he invited all of the Red Wings to sit in the front row of his concert at Detroit's Cobo Hall. He had a case of beer placed in front of every seat, and he invited us all backstage to talk to him a few minutes before the concert began.

One guy who is exactly the same as his public image is McEnroe. Tracee and I have been friends with John and his wife, Patty, for 20 years. Our kids have grown up together, attending the same sports camps during the summer.

I can testify that McEnroe still has the burning passion that made him a champion on the court. I love it when he gets fired up, which can happen often. He strives to be the best no matter what he does. He can't turn it off.

Once, he asked me to officiate at an exhibition match. When he didn't like some of my calls, he said, "If you are going to do it, do it right!"

I walked off the court but we remain good friends. That's just who John is.

At my induction, Cuba Gooding Jr. told the media that he first met me when I elbowed him in the corner during a celebrity hockey game. Though I don't remember it, that's probably true.

The only person I wished had been at my induction who wasn't was my ex-Blackhawks teammate Gary Suter. It was perfect that we were able to go into the U.S. Hockey Hall of Fame together. The induction ceremony was in Chicago that year, making it even better. Given Suter's quiet nature, I was predicting disaster when he got up to make his speech at that event. I told him his speech was going to be the worst in the history of the Hall of Fame. But Suter hit it out of the park, saying the right words and thanking the right people.

Two years later, when I was elected to the Hockey Hall of Fame, I invited Suter to be there with me as my favorite teammate.

"Sorry, I won't go to Canada," Suter said. "Not going back there."

He was still worried about what Canadians might do to him because he hurt Gretzky at the Canada Cup, even though that happened almost 30 years ago. I couldn't be too upset by his decision; that was the nervous Suter that we all knew and loved.

EVERYTHING I HAVE TODAY, I owe to hockey. I have tried not to forget those who have helped me along the way.

My friendship with Russell Lowell has endured through the years. He has carved out his own niche as a prominent chef. At one point, he was cooking for Microsoft kingpin Bill Gates.

Now my Malibu crew knows Russell as well. And as he likes to say, whenever we get together trouble usually follows, even today.

Russell is also in the process of writing a book that will include a story about how he cooked up a mule deer that had been struck by a car near the entrance to Pepperdine University. The story starts with the sad passing of our San Diego friend James O'Connell. Although Russell rearranged his schedule to attend the funeral, he told me that he didn't have time for a lengthy visit. He had to get back to his home in the state of Washington for a cooking engagement.

The funeral was a sad affair, and it wasn't the kind of send-off we would have liked to see for our friend. I asked Russell to stay an extra day so we could remember the good times with O'Connell.

Given Russell's expertise in food, I picked the trendy Nobu restaurant. We sat at a table with actors Jeremy Piven, Dustin Hoffman, Mark Wahlberg, and a couple of stunt women.

The women mentioned a party afterward, but it was a celebrity fest and the paparazzi were everywhere. I had no desire to see my photo ending up in the *National Enquirer*. We decided to head for my house.

As we neared Pepperdine, Russell spotted the 180-pound mule deer stumbling around just after it had been struck by a car.

"We need to stop," Russell said.

"There is nothing we can do," I said.

"Yes, there is," he said.

Knowing it wasn't possible to transport the deer home in my car, we eventually went to my house to get my truck. It was after 2:00 AM and I woke up my son Dean and asked him to help us. He said we were crazy and went back to bed. That's when I decided to call Cusack, who just happened to be driving home from a party. Cusack also has Chicago roots, and started following my career when I was with the Blackhawks. In 2009, when I was playing my last NHL season, Cusack was quoted in *Sports Illustrated* as saying that I "was the oldest man in the world. He's actually 792 years old." We've had good times together.

Cusack met us at the accident site. We loaded the now-dead deer in the truck and took it back to my garage, where Russell butchered it with the skill of a surgeon. He turned the deer into steaks. He noted during the process that none of the meat had been bruised by the accident.

The only problem was that we made a mess. Blood was splattered all over the garage and kitchen. My Malibu home looked like a crime scene.

When Tracee woke up around 6:00 AM she was not pleased with what had transpired.

"Don't even look in the refrigerator," Russell told Tracee. "We will get it cleaned up."

When the butchering was complete, we still had the deer head and other remains and no idea how to dispose of them. We decided the best plan was to bury them at sea. We dragged the carcass and head to the beach and let the tide carry them out. I figured some fish would dine well that day.

The next morning one of my Malibu neighbors, billionaire Don Wildman, saw me outside and waved me over to excitedly tell me an incredible tale about how he found a deer's head on his beach.

Other neighbors had gathered as he theorized that the deer had walked into the surf and a shark had come into the shallow water and attacked it. I listened to him tell the story for a while, and then I told him what really happened.

Later that day, Russell grilled up the venison medallions, and none of our guests had any idea they were eating road kill.

You know you have a friend for life when you butcher a deer with them.

TO BE HONEST, THE entire induction weekend was overwhelming. It was a blur of people and conversations. You hope you remember to thank everyone. You hope you say the appropriate words. You hope people understand how much you have appreciated their friendship and their help during your career.

You are told to limit your speech to about 20 minutes, meaning it's impossible to thank everyone meaningful in your life.

The only regret I had about my speech was not taking the time to point out that Gretzky was the greatest ambassador the NHL has ever had or will have. He was a great player and is a wonderful man. He has been the perfect face of our sport.

I hope what people took from my speech is that I felt fortunate to have played hockey as long as I did. The path I took to the NHL may have been comical, but I was very serious about being a top player.

When I look back at my playing days, what I'm most proud of is the fact that most of my teammates would say I was a good team guy. What I liked best about playing hockey were the guys. I loved the feeling I got when everyone worked together to achieve a common objective. The best teams are those where the players play for each other, not for themselves.

I also want to be remembered as a player who just liked to play hockey. I didn't go to Moose Jaw to attract the notice of the NHL. I went to Moose Jaw to keep playing a sport I loved to play.

After my final NHL game for the Atlanta Thrashers in 2010, I reported back to the Chicago Wolves to play in the AHL play-offs. I joked that I was going out on the bottom, not the top. But maybe it was appropriate that I ended my career in the AHL, because it was a reminder that I played all of those years not because I loved the glory but because I loved playing.

Cusack attended one of my final games with the Wolves, and I ended up getting two teeth chipped while he was watching. He was surprised that I was still willing to go out after the game. To me, dental issues were hardly a cause for great concern. You see the dentist and you fix the problem.

In an interview with Yahoo.com at my induction, Cusack seemed bemused by how enthused I was to be playing in the minor leagues.

"He was with all these minor leaguers," Cusack said. "It could have been a sad story, but it wasn't, because he took his show there. 'This is what I do.' It was sort of amazing. He was this Hall of Famer, clearly, amongst these kids, and they were running him and doing all these things, and he's like, 'I play hockey.'"

That is what I want people to remember about me.

The most important person at my induction was probably Parker, who had recommended me to Coach Billows in the first place.

Without Parker giving me the coach's number, I may never have gotten beyond rec-league hockey.

Through the years, we have kept in touch. I have always felt as if I owed him thanks for that telephone number and for having my back in my two seasons in Moose Jaw. Hockey in that era was wild and brawl-filled, and you couldn't survive unless your teammates had your back.

And yes, I remembered what Parker had said to me in our last playoff game together. I didn't understand his meaning until he told me he was losing his eyesight.

At the end of the induction weekend, when I was saying good-bye to Parker, I thanked him for what he did for my career.

"You said that I had to play for both of us," I reminded him. "And I got us both all the way to the Hall of Fame."

As it turned out, my game plan in hockey was the same one we had surfing 30 years in San Diego. I caught a big wave and rode it as hard as I could for as long as I could.

Acknowledgments

O ccasionally you hear it said that an athlete came out of nowhere to become a star player.

But a guy from nowhere probably had more visibility than I had playing beer league hockey in San Diego, California. My climb from beach bum to Hall of Fame hockey player has to be one of the more unlikely journeys in sports history.

I would like to acknowledge the late Jim Perner and his family for the effort they made to get me ice time in Chicago when I was a young player. Jim bought used taxis, pulled off the decals, and used those vehicles to drive us wherever we needed to go to find a rink. Sometimes it was after midnight. Once, a fellow put a rink in a barn and we skated there for three hours.

With my dad working all of the time at his restaurant, I don't know whether I would have developed as a hockey player without the help of the Perner family.

Likewise, I owe a huge thanks to Pat Doyle for paying my way to Mount Carmel High School in Chicago. At that point in my life, I needed that level of education and hockey competition.

I probably owe my entire NHL career to former Moose Jaw Canucks coach Larry Billows. If he hadn't taken a chance on me, I probably never would have advanced beyond the San Diego beer leagues.

I also owe major thanks to my Moose Jaw defensive partner Bobby Parker, the guy who gave me Billows' phone number on a San Diego beach. Parker had my back while I was learning how to be a defenseman. He also provided several of the Moose Jaw stories that were included in this book.

Thanks also to my San Diego buddy Russell Lowell and my Moose Jaw teammate Wendal Jellison for contributing tales from long ago.

While I'm passing out thanks, I want to express my gratitude to former Wisconsin assistant coach Grant Standbrook for transforming me into a defenseman. The always-serious Standbrook taught me more about playing defense than anyone in my career.

The late Wisconsin coach Bob Johnson was also important to my success. I already had passion, but he was a positive influence at a time when I needed one. His replacement, Jeff Sauer, also provided positive reinforcement.

I also want to thank the late Herb Brooks and the members of the 1980 U.S. Olympic team for helping pave the way for me to play in the NHL. What they did for American hockey cannot be underestimated.

Thanks also to Bob Gainey and Larry Robinson for showing me how to be a professional player in Montreal. Larry was always there for me, no matter how things were going for me. Robinson made me feel comfortable in a foreign city. The same was true about Craig Ludwig. He was a laid-back player who cared far more than he ever showed. Ludwig loved playing the game but always acted like he didn't.

Former Montreal coach Jacques Lemaire also taught me much about the game, but truth be told he scared the hell out of me. He intimidated me. He was very stern. His eyes would look right through me.

As much as I appreciated the learning experiences I had with other coaches, I probably thrived most under the tougher coaching style of Mike Keenan. On the ice, he pushed me to be a stronger, tougher, grittier player. He helped me take my game to another level.

Keenan also provided information and stories for this book, as did my former Chicago Blackhawks teammate Jeremy Roenick. Their contributions are appreciated.

I also want to thank the Ilitch family, general manager Ken Holland, and the Red Wings organization for the treatment I've received in Detroit. I've now been with this team a long time, and I have always been treated well.

I love how the Ilitch family stands up for the city of Detroit and its teams. Mike and Marian Ilitch are a shining example of living the American dream. They started with one pizza stand, and look where they are today. What I like most about them is that they climbed to the top with class and dignity, their morals and ethics intact.

Thanks to Mitch Rogatz and Triumph Books for giving me the opportunity to tell my story. Thanks also to Adam Motin for his editorial expertise.

Away from the ice, I need to thank Chicago native John-Andrew Kambanis, who was a member of the 1998 and 2002 Greek bobsled team. He gave me the opportunity to dabble in bobsledding during the 2004–05 NHL lockout. Accomplished surfer Laird Hamilton and I both traveled to Lake Placid, New York, with the idea that we might be able to add a second sport to our résumés.

I had no illusions about being a bobsled driver. That requires far more experience and training than we could acquire in the time we had. But members of the four-man bobsled who do the pushing at the start usually have a track background. I had always been fast and had strength in my legs. I had the requisite agility. I thought if I worked at it, I could become a quality bobsledder.

Hamilton hurt his shoulder in our training session, and that was it for him. But I competed with the Greek team at the America's Cup that year in Calgary, Alberta. It was an Olympic qualifying event for lower-rung competitors such as Greece, Jamaica, and Mexico.

I have never laughed as hard as I did when I saw the Mexican team drive up with its sled in the bed of an El Camino. They had made the trip all the way up from Mexico.

Because of the movie *Cool Runnings*, people think of the Jamaican team as being kind of a joke. But they seemed well trained, and the Jamaicans were among the top competitors in this competition.

The Greek sled made three runs and we flipped over twice. Of course, the only photo of the event published in the Calgary newspaper was our sled sliding down the course on its side.

When you crash, the objective is to keep your head off the track, presumably to prevent a serious head injury. But we spilled early, and I was flying down the ice on my shoulder. It was burning from the friction. At one point, I had to place my helmet on the ice just to provide some relief. When I was at the bottom of the run, I saw that the friction had burned a hole in my helmet.

For some reason, Canadian Olympic gold medal bobsledder Pierre Lueders decided to rip me for my decision to compete in his sport. He said my efforts were "ridiculous" and "utter nonsense."

I got the last laugh. I told the media that I didn't understand why Lueders was upset considering that he had loaned me his equipment to compete. The truth was that I had simply pulled gear out of his locker in Calgary.

We had no success in Calgary, finishing last out of nine teams. I came away from my bobsledding experience impressed with the athletes who compete in that sport. I have said that making a bobsled run is like compressing all of the intensity and physicality of a hockey game into a one-minute span. You get banged around quite a bit during a run.

Despite what Lueders said, I believe I could have been a quality bobsledder, given the proper training.

I HOPE THIS BOOK makes it clear that I value my family greatly and that I appreciate the contributions and sacrifices they have made for my career.

The reason I dedicated the book to my late sister Gigi is that she enjoyed my career more than anybody. She enjoyed being my sister and working at Cheli's Chili Bar in Chicago. When she was coping with cancer, that job kept her going. If you ask anyone who went in there, they will remember how much she loved being in the inner circle when I was with the Blackhawks.

My sister Penny also worked there, and many fans have stories about how well Penny treated them when they stopped by the restaurant. A fan once called right after we closed, and Penny waited until the fan arrived and re-opened the place to give her a tour. My sisters were wonderful goodwill ambassadors.

The first time I walked into the Montreal Canadiens dressing room for a Sunday practice and saw that players had brought their kids into the dressing room, I couldn't wait to have my own kids.

I knew the experience of bringing up children in the hockey family environment would be memorable, but it exceeded all my expectations.

It's not easy being the son or daughter of a professional athlete, but my children handled it with pride, dignity, and respect. When I played, the best compliments I ever received were about how well behaved my children were.

It was particularly challenging for my sons, Dean and Jake, when they played youth hockey. They heard trash talking on the ice and from the stands that they should not have heard, but they handled it as well as could be expected.

But I take no credit for raising great children. That credit goes to my wife, Tracee. She is an exceptional parent. She has kept the family grounded while I focused on my career. Through several moves and countless upheavals, Tracee has been the key player in our family. I always say my wife is bulletproof. That is a requirement if you are married to me.

Tracee and I have different approaches to life but she always knows when to be sympathetic to my position and when to tell me I'm wrong. I listen to her advice far more than she thinks I do. By admitting that it this book, I have showed her my hand. That is going to cost me.

Few people know that on the day we were married, my parents tried to convince me to call off the wedding. Tracee and my dad didn't get along, and my parents believed they were trying to protect me.

Tracee and her bridal party hadn't yet arrived at the church, and I can vividly recall my parents making their case that I should stay single. (We were doing shots at the time, so that should explain everything.)

Tired of their arguments, I asked my father to give me one good reason why I shouldn't marry Tracee.

"She is too short," my father said.

"But she is taller than Mom," I said.

It's one of the few times I've stopped my father right in his tracks. He had nothing to say.

On that day, I made the right decision by marrying Tracee. I've made some bad choices during my career, but that was not one of them.

WHILE WRITING THIS BOOK I realized that I sometimes sound as I though I hate Canada and the Canadian fans, but that couldn't be further from the truth. Canada is where I got my break, both in junior hockey and in the NHL. The truth is that after all the battles my U.S. teams had against Canada, I simply became frustrated with losing. I'm a sore loser, so I did what came naturally to me—I argued and fought and acted out toward Canadians. Let me be clear: if it wasn't for hockey I wouldn't have a bad word to say about Canada. In my eyes, Canadians take the game a little too seriously. But if it wasn't for the pride they took in hockey, I would have never turned out the way I did. So, thanks, Canada, for the attitude. And go USA!

Finally, thank you to everyone who played a role in my career. There are tons of people I would like to thank if I had the space here. Rest assured that not a day goes by where I don't think back on how lucky I was to have the support of my friends and family. From the frozen park in Evergreen Park where it all started to where I am now, it's been one wild ride.

Mom, Dad, thank you and I love you for all you've done for me.

Gigi, Penny, Eleni, and Steve, I hope I made you guys proud of your brother.

Tracee, Dean, Jake, Caley, and Tara, you guys are the only thing I love more than hockey. I am so proud of all of you!

I still say hockey is the greatest sport in the world, not just because the game itself is great but because of the quality of character of the people involved.

Thank you, everyone!